W9-BEQ-522
des 6-8 (don)
logan

CHARACTER EDUCATION

INSTRUCTION • ACTIVITIES • ASSESSMENT

A Gift to students in Teacher Education from their
Federations: ETFO, OECTA & OSSTF (2009)

Donated by

TELC

Centre de ressources de la Faculté d'éducation
Université d'Ottawa - University of Ottawa
Faculty of Education Resource Centre

Published by World Teachers Press®

www.worldteacherspress.com

Published with the permission of R.I.C. Publications Pty. Ltd.

Copyright © 2006 by Didax, Inc., Rowley, MA 01969. All rights reserved.

First published by R.I.C. Publications Pty. Ltd., Perth, Western Australia. Revised by Didax Educational Resources.

Limited reproduction permission: The publisher grants permission to individual teachers who have purchased this book to reproduce the blackline masters as needed for use with their own students. Reproduction for an entire school or school district or for commercial use is prohibited.

Printed in the United States of America.

This book is printed on recycled paper.

Order Number 2-5266
ISBN 978-1-58324-243-8

D E F G H 12 11 10 09 08

372.0114
.C433
2006

395 Main Street
Rowley, MA 01969
vww.didax.com

Character Education

Character Education introduces and develops the knowledge, skills, attitudes and values that will help students lead healthy and fulfilling lives. Students will consider what it means to be healthy—socially, mentally and emotionally—and will be given experiences to assist them to become responsible, caring members of society.

The book focuses on character building and values. Most experts agree that people with defined values and a good self-image are better equipped to deal with challenging situations. The activities encourage students to consider their own values and develop a sense of self-worth. It also focuses on the importance of showing respect for and tolerance towards others and valuing diversity in our society.

Character Education provides a comprehensive coverage of values content, supports teachers in planning and implementing lessons and, through collaborative learning and thoughtful discussion, promotes a lifelong commitment to a healthy value base.

> **Other titles in this series:**
>
> *Character Education, Grades 2-4*
>
> *Character Education, Grades 6-8*

Contents

Teacher Information

Character Education focuses on character building and values. The activities encourage students to consider their own values and develop a sense of self-worth. It also focuses on the importance of showing respect and tolerance towards others and valuing diversity in our society.

The notes on the following pages provide comprehensive information about terms and concepts used in this book.

A teacher notes page accompanies each student worksheet. It provides the following information:

Specific indicators explain what the students are expected to demonstrate through completing the activities.

Discussion points have been suggested to further develop ideas on the student worksheet. They can also encourage the students to comprehend, assess and form opinions about what they have read.

What to do gives suggested step-by-step instructions for the activity. The accompanying worksheet may be the focus of the activity or it may be where the students record their ideas after completing a task or discussion.

Answers to all worksheet activities are included. Some answers will need a teacher check, while others will vary depending on the students' personal experiences, opinions, etc.

Additional activities can be used to further develop the outcomes being assessed. These activities provide ideas to consolidate and clarify the concepts and skills taught in the activity.

Background information has been included to enhance your understanding of the concept being taught and to provide additional information to relate to the students.

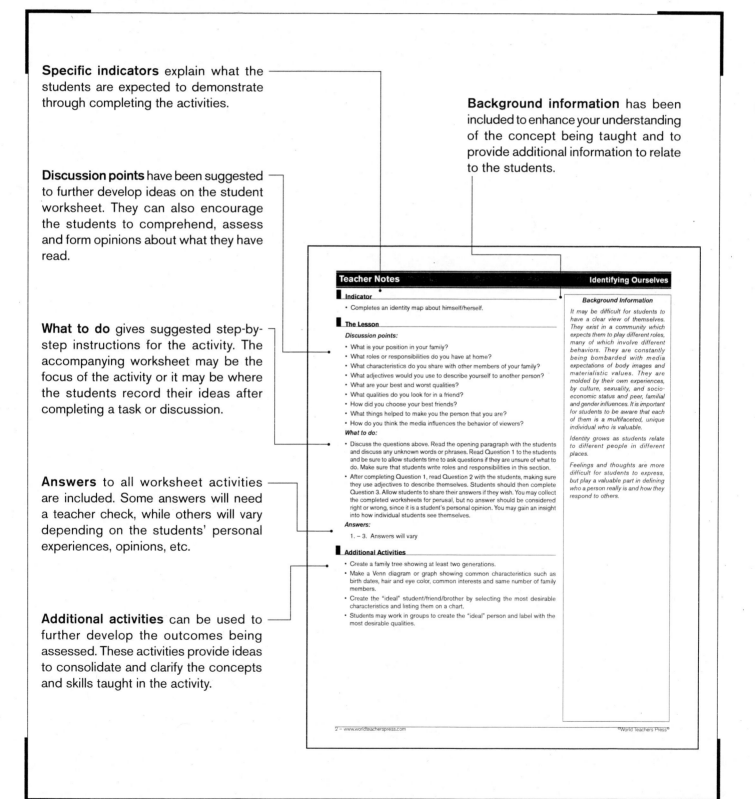

Teacher Notes **Identifying Ourselves**

Indicator

- Completes an identity map about himself/herself.

The Lesson

Discussion points:

- What is your position in your family?
- What roles or responsibilities do you have at home?
- What characteristics do you share with other members of your family?
- What adjectives would you use to describe yourself to another person?
- What are your best and worst qualities?
- What qualities do you look for in a friend?
- How did you choose your best friends?
- What things helped to make you the person that you are?
- How do you think the media influences the behavior of viewers?

What to do:

- Discuss the questions above. Read the opening paragraph with the students and discuss any unknown words or phrases. Read Question 1 to the students and be sure to allow students time to ask questions if they are unsure of what to do. Make sure that students write roles and responsibilities in this section.
- After completing Question 1, read Question 2 with the students, making sure they use adjectives to describe themselves. Students should then complete Question 3. Allow students to share their answers if they wish. You may collect the completed worksheets for perusal, but no answer should be considered right or wrong, since it is a student's personal opinion. You may gain an insight into how individual students see themselves.

Answers:

1. – 3. Answers will vary

Additional Activities

- Create a family tree showing at least two generations.
- Make a Venn diagram or graph showing common characteristics such as birth dates, hair and eye color, common interests and same number of family members.
- Create the "ideal" student/friend/brother by selecting the most desirable characteristics and listing them on a chart.
- Students may work in groups to create the "ideal" person and label with the most desirable qualities.

Background Information

It may be difficult for students to have a clear view of themselves. They exist in a community which expects them to play different roles, many of which involve different behaviors. They are constantly being bombarded with media expectations of body images and materialistic values. They are molded by their own experiences, by culture, sexuality, and socio-economic status and peer, familial and gender influences. It is important for students to be aware that each of them is a multifaceted, unique individual who is valuable.

Identity grows as students relate to different people in different places.

Feelings and thoughts are more difficult for students to express, but play a valuable part in defining who a person really is and how they respond to others.

2 – www.worldteacherspress.com   ©World Teachers Press®

Character Education–Book 3 ©World Teachers Press®

Teacher Information

A variety of student worksheets is provided, which may contain a selection of role-plays to perform; scenarios to read and consider; information to read, discuss and answer questions about; or values or feelings to consider and compare with others.

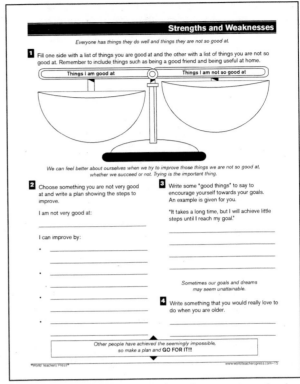

Student activities to reinforce and develop understanding of the concept.

Questioning activities where students are required to consider and evaluate personal feelings or values.

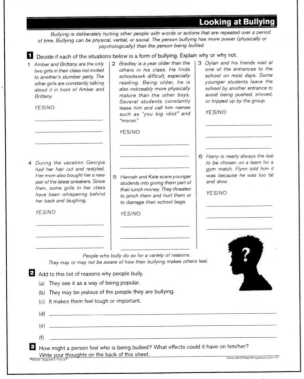

Several pages provide a selection of role-plays or scenarios for students to use in a variety of ways.

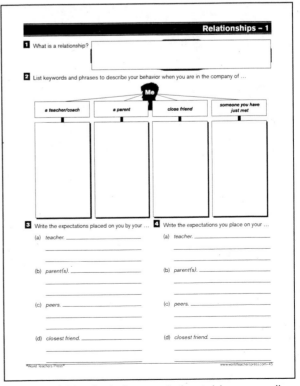

Other activities include completing tables or reading and labeling diagrams.

Suggestions for Teaching Character Education

Character Education introduces and develops the knowledge, skills, attitudes and values that will enable students to lead healthy and fulfilling lives. Students will consider what it means to be healthy—socially, mentally and emotionally—and will be given the tools to become responsible, caring members of society.

Many of the activities in this book provide students with an opportunity to formulate their thoughts on a topic and express their opinions and feelings. Classroom discussions are valuable for encouraging critical and reflective thinking.

▌Teaching Character Education

- Create a safe atmosphere in the classroom so students feel they can share their thoughts and feelings.
- Identify what it is the students are going to take away from the lesson. (Refer to the "Indicator" in the Teacher Notes for each activity.)
- Begin with a discussion or, with older students, a hypothetical situation. (Refer to the "Discussion points" in the Teacher Notes for each activity.)
- Listen to and be honest with the students. (Give something of yourself. Share some of your own experiences, where appropriate.)
- Show respect for the students' thoughts and feelings.
- Be non-judgmental.

In your responses, encourage students to analyze their statements by asking such things as "What could happen if you did that?" or "Who else would be affected by that?" rather than giving your own opinion.

With some topics, students may make suggestions where you can respond "Is that the RIGHT thing to do?" Such a question can promote discussions regarding individual, group, community and global values. Who is it "right" for?

Although students should feel free to express their opinions, it is important that they understand there is a "right" conclusion, rather than letting them think whatever they conclude is correct.

▌Creating a Safe Atmosphere

For an effective values lesson to take place, students need to feel comfortable enough to share their thoughts, feelings, opinions and past experiences. They need to feel there will be no ridicule, no put-downs and a non-judgmental atmosphere.

One way to promote this safe atmosphere during discussions with younger students is to make the effort to sit the students in a circle, even if it means going to another room to do this. Some schools call this time "circle time." Set clear rules, such as one student speaking at a time and no put-downs or making faces. Make the circle a safe place where the students feel comfortable to talk openly about their feelings, worries and achievements.

Students can be encouraged to become respectful listeners. Ensure that students raise their hands if they wish to make a comment; or, for younger students, an item can be placed in the middle of the circle such as a "talking stick" or small toy. Only students holding this are able to speak.

Explain to the class that many people only "half listen" as they are thinking about what they might say when the speaker stops. Some people don't even wait for the speaker to stop, and interrupt him or her in the middle of a sentence. During "circle time," teachers and students have the opportunity to share their thoughts without being interrupted.

It is important for students to understand that personal issues discussed during these open forum meetings are not to become topics of conversation outside the classroom. You will also need to show respect to the students unless, of course, issues are raised involving abuse or that need attention by parents. You will then need to consult his/her principal regarding any action that needs to be taken.

Once the class has a routine set in place to discuss issues openly and respectfully, these skills can be transferred to discussions about issues affecting the class, such as conflict and bullying.

 ©World Teachers Press®

Suggestions for Teaching Character Education

Values Education

Most definitions agree that "values" are those qualities which an individual or a society considers to be important as principles for conduct.

The *Character Education* series helps students to consider their personal strengths and weaknesses and reinforces the advantages of having a strong set of values.

A person's set of values affects his or her thinking and behavior. When people are confident in themselves and have strong values, it is easier to do things that are "right." Those who have weaker values can often be led easily and may do things they don't really want to do.

You can encourage students to have a positive self-image through praise and by recognizing individual achievements.

You can foster the development of personal qualities such as perseverance, kindness, and dealing with stress and criticism. You can also discuss some values with students, such as honesty, generosity and tolerance. You might also like to discuss other things people may value, like pets, music and the environment.

Tolerance and Empathy

Tolerance and empathy should be encouraged in students. Activities such as drama games, which require students to put themselves in someone else's place and imagine how that person feels, can help to foster empathy. Tolerance is an ongoing process that teaches students not to hate. You can teach tolerance most effectively by modeling tolerant behavior in the classroom and on the playground, ensuring students are exposed to multicultural literature and images, and teaching them about various faiths, ethnicities and lifestyles. Educating students to be tolerant will:

- Promote the understanding and acceptance of individual differences.
- Promote the idea that differences can enhance our relationships and enrich our society.
- Minimize generalizations and stereotyping.
- Promote the need to combat prejudice and discrimination.

This book emphasizes the importance of respecting the feelings and emotions of others. It uses scenarios to help students "put themselves in the shoes" of others. When students develop empathy for others, the dynamics of situations can change.

Collaborative Learning

When students are able to work together in groups, they are encouraged to communicate and express their ideas. It is important that you monitor groups working independently to ensure that all students are working together as a team. By assigning a role for each group member, it is more likely that the dynamics will be equitable. The roles of the students can be swapped regularly to give each member the opportunity to participate in all tasks.

Allow time at the end of the group tasks for the students to evaluate their team skills and to make targets to work towards the next time they form as a group. Some activities may work better if the groups are organized by ability levels, others will be enriched by mixed-ability groupings. To enable all students to work together at some stage during the year, randomly select groups for some activities.

Differentiating Activities

The activities in the *Character Education* series have been designed so they can be followed precisely or adapted by teachers. This flexibility allows you the opportunity to modify lessons and worksheets to meet the needs of students with varying abilities and special needs.

To meet the special needs of English as a second language (ESL) students or those who have low levels of literacy, plan a time to introduce keywords and concepts. Having other adult support is ideal as the group can work in a quiet area away from the classroom. Keywords can be enlarged and discussed. Being immersed in the language before a topic begins gives these students an advantage, especially during the teacher discussion part of the lesson, when most teachers tend to speak quite quickly.

If other adults are not available, mixed-ability groups will allow ESL students and students with low literacy levels to observe and be guided by other students.

Students who seem to "race" through the activities and worksheets and who understand the content very quickly can be challenged by looking at the topic in greater depth (rather than being given more of the same). They can go beyond the facts and conduct research related to strands of the topics that interest them.

By meeting the needs of individual students, allowing the students to learn collaboratively and by having very clear instructions and expectations, values lessons should run smoothly.

Assessment Indicators

Below are the indicators from the activity pages of *Character Education, Grades 6-8*. These indicators can be transferred across to the assessment form on page 10. By using forms, you can meet the needs of outcome-based learning experiences in values education. The format of each page is ideal for inclusion in student portfolios or for reporting purposes. Using forms allows you to provide a well-explained, logically-presented indication of progress to both students and parents. Indicators have been developed as a basis for determining progress towards achieving outcomes.

Pages 12 – 13
- Completes an identity map about himself/herself.

Pages 14 – 15
- Understands the terms "role" and "responsibilities."
- Identifies own roles and responsibilities within different groups.
- Comments on how he/she carries out each role and suggests personal improvements.

Pages 16 – 17
- Recognizes personal feelings related to given statements.

Pages 18 – 19
- Recognizes personal feelings related to given statements.

Pages 20 – 21
- Considers the importance of self-worth.

Pages 22 – 23
- Shows an understanding of self-esteem.
- Considers some ways self-esteem is influenced.

Pages 24 – 25
- Identifies strengths and weaknesses.
- Identifies steps to achieve a goal.
- Writes phrases to provide encouragement towards achieving a goal.

Pages 26 – 27
- Selects strategies to develop self-esteem.
- Writes positive statements or words about himself/herself.
- Compares descriptions about himself/herself.

Pages 28 – 29
- Identifies strategies to improve his/her own self-esteem.
- Uses "I" statements to demonstrate positive self-worth.
- Demonstrates possible situations in which he/she could take a risk.

Pages 30 – 31
- Identifies how he/she responds to different situations.
- Discusses and practices possible responses to different situations.
- Uses "I" statements with confidence to demonstrate assertive behavior.

Pages 32 – 33
- Generates personal goals which are based on being fit and active.
- Devises strategies to attain his/her personal goals.
- Evaluates his/her decisions in the process of setting personal goals.

Pages 34 – 35
- Generates personal goals which are based on being fit and active.
- Devises strategies to attain his/her personal goals.
- Evaluates his/her decisions in the process of setting personal goals.

Pages 36 – 37
- Identifies events that cause stress.
- Identifies activities that aid relaxation.
- Completes an action plan to combat stress.
- Completes a simple time management format.

Pages 38 – 39
- Understands some ways in which stress can be managed.
- Considers how he/she deals with stress.

Pages 40 – 41
- Evaluates current time management practices.
- Establishes time management strategies which incorporate aspects of a healthy lifestyle.

Pages 42 – 43
- Gains an understanding of the term "fair play."
- Values fair play.

Pages 44 – 45
- Participates in teamwork activities requiring cooperation and communication.
- Identifies the qualities of good teamwork.
- Evaluates teamwork performance of his/her group.

Pages 46 – 47
- Understands what is meant by "effective communication."
- Considers how well he/she communicates with others.

Pages 48 – 49
- Understands the importance of family.
- Considers the relationships within his/her own family.

Pages 50 – 51
- Reviews current and past friendships.
- Evaluates himself/herself as a person in order to develop friendships.
- Establishes strategies to make new friendships while maintaining existing friendships.

Pages 52 – 53
- Reviews current and past friendships.
- Evaluates what characteristics are important to him/her.
- Establishes strategies to make new friendships and maintain existing friendships.

Pages 54 – 57
- Explores different types of relationships: child/parent, child/teacher, child/child.
- Identifies different standards of behavior in different relationships.
- Identifies the expectations placed on him/her in different relationships.

Pages 58 – 59
- Completes questions about empathy.
- Interviews another student to gain some understanding of his/her feelings, attitudes, likes and dislikes.

Pages 60 – 61
- Gains an understanding of the types of expectations and assumptions people can have about boys and girls.
- Considers what effects these expectations and assumptions can have on people's lives.

Pages 62 – 63
- Understands the meaning of the term "stereotype."
- Identifies and describes stereotypes in real life and on television.
- Realizes the way people are treated according to a stereotype can affect their self-concept.

Pages 64 – 65
- Understands the meaning of the word "stereotype."
- Considers stereotypes in his/her community.
- Considers the meaning of the word "empathy."

Pages 66 – 67
- Considers the positive and negative effects peer pressure has on influencing behavior and self-concept.

Assessment Indicators

Pages 68 – 69	• Considers the negative effects peer pressure has on influencing behavior and self-concept.
Pages 70 – 71	• Identifies and categorizes scenarios into those that are bullying and those that are not.
Pages 72 – 73	• Understands what the term "bullying" means. • Identifies examples of physical, verbal and social bullying. • Considers the possible consequences of bullying. • Uses role-play to demonstrate different strategies for dealing with bullying.
Pages 74 – 75	• Uses conflict resolution steps to find solutions to scenarios.
Pages 76 – 77	• Understands and discusses steps to resolve conflicts in a mutually acceptable way.
Pages 78 – 79	• Reads and discusses conflict resolution scenarios.
Pages 80 – 83	• Identifies and describes tolerant and intolerant behavior.
Pages 84 – 87	• Recognizes actions that are disrespectful. • Considers ways to act respectfully toward others. • Identifies ways of showing respect to other people.
Pages 88 – 89	• Considers possible consequences in taking risks.
Pages 90 – 91	• Follows decision-making steps to make a decision.
Pages 92 – 93	• Understands and uses a plan to make decisions. • Considers some important decisions he/she has made.
Pages 94 – 97	• Understands the meaning of values. • Identifies some of his/her own values.
Pages 98 – 99	• Reads a poem about keeping the environment healthy. • Offers suggestions about how to keep the environment healthy.
Pages 100 – 101	• Demonstrates an understanding that commitment to a project is part of being responsible. • Considers carefully a project he/she would like to participate in and plans his/her involvement in detail.
Pages 102 – 103	• Describes actions to address an issue affecting the environment.

Using the Assessment Form (page 10)

An explanation of how to use the form.

Task(s) • Give a brief description of the activity and what was expected of the students.

Assessment • Write the relevant indicator(s) as listed above and assess appropriately.

Teacher Comment • Use this space to comment on aspects of an individual student's performance which cannot be indicated in the formal assessment, such as work habits or particular needs or abilities.

Using the Skills and Attitudes Assessment Form (page 11)

An explanation of how to use the form.

Assessment • Assess the specific development of an individual student in these areas.

Teacher Comments • Use this space to comment on an individual student's skills and attitudes.

Assessment Form

Name _____ **Grade** _____ **Term** _____

Task(s)
The student was asked to:

Assessment
The student:

	Demonstrated	Needs further opportunity

Teacher Comments

_____
_____
_____
_____
_____
_____
_____

Character Education–Book 3 ©World Teachers Press®

Assessment Form – Skills and Attitudes

Name

Name

Grade

Term

Assessment

The student:	Demonstrated	Needs further opportunity
• appreciates the need for safe practices in a range of situations		
• strives to achieve the best results in personal performance		
• manages his/her time effectively		
• makes decisions for himself/herself		
• shows an understanding of fair play		
• participates in and enjoys group activities		
• works cooperatively to complete a task		
• recognizes his/her weaknesses and works to improve them		
• sets goals for himself/herself		
• achieves goals for himself/herself		
• communicates effectively		
• listens effectively		
• makes and maintains positive relationships		
• appreciates the similarities and differences between himself/herself and others		
• shows sensitivity and tolerance towards others		
• shows respect for others		
• has a positive self-image		
• recognizes the need for balance among physical, emotional and social health		

Teacher Comments

Indicator

• Completes an identity map about himself/herself.

The Lesson

Discussion points:

• What is your position in your family?

• What roles or responsibilities do you have at home?

• What characteristics do you share with other members of your family?

• What adjectives would you use to describe yourself to another person?

• What are your best and worst qualities?

• What qualities do you look for in a friend?

• How did you choose your best friends?

• What things helped to make you the person that you are?

• How do you think the media influences the behavior of viewers?

What to do:

• Discuss the questions above. Read the opening paragraph with the students and discuss any unknown words or phrases. Read Question 1 to the students and be sure to allow students time to ask questions if they are unsure of what to do. Make sure that students write roles and responsibilities in this section.

• After completing Question 1, read Question 2 with the students, making sure they use adjectives to describe themselves. Students should then complete Question 3. Allow students to share their answers if they wish. You may collect the completed worksheets for perusal, but no answer should be considered right or wrong, since it is a student's personal opinion. You may gain an insight into how individual students see themselves.

Answers:

Answers will vary

Additional Activities

• Create a family tree showing at least two generations.

• Make a Venn diagram or graph showing common characteristics such as birth dates, hair and eye color, common interests and same number of family members.

• Create the "ideal" student/friend/brother by selecting the most desirable characteristics and listing them on a chart.

• Students may work in groups to create the "ideal" person and label with the most desirable qualities.

Background Information

It may be difficult for students to have a clear view of themselves. They exist in a community which expects them to play different roles, many of which involve different behaviors. They are constantly being bombarded with media expectations of body images and materialistic values. They are molded by their own experiences, by culture, sexuality, and socio-economic status and peer, familial and gender influences. It is important for students to be aware that each of them is a multifaceted, unique individual who is valuable.

Identity grows as students relate to different people in different places.

Feelings and thoughts are more difficult for students to express, but play a valuable part in defining who a person really is and how they respond to others.

No two people are the same. We look, think and behave differently. Each of us is unique and special.
Our identity is defined by our family, our friends, our cultural background, our hobbies and interests, our likes and dislikes, our experiences, and our values and beliefs.

1 Use the map below to represent aspects of your identity. You should include roles or responsibilities that you have such as brother, nephew, grandson, friend, goalkeeper, student, student council member, etc.

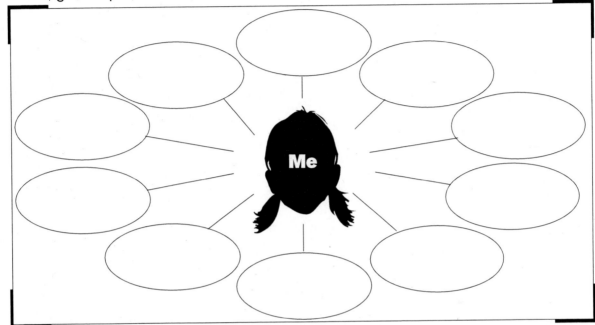

2 Repeat the activity, but this time include character traits, such as loyal, funny, friendly, short-tempered, creative, etc.

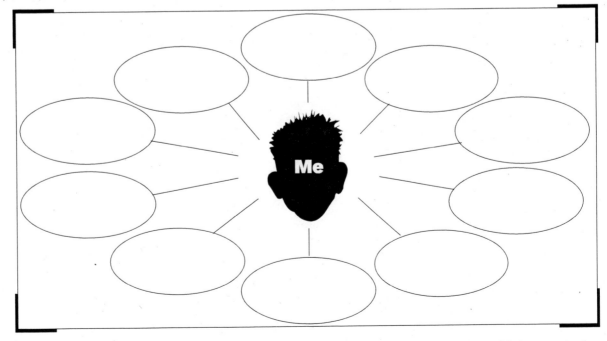

3 Compare your answers to those of someone else. Draw a cross out on any traits which are similar and circle any traits which are different.

Indicators

- Understands the terms "role" and "responsibilities."
- Identifies own roles and responsibilities within different groups.
- Comments on how he/she carries out each role and suggests personal improvements.

The Lesson

Discussion points:

- What is a "role"?
- What is meant by "responsibility"?
- Discuss roles and responsibilities of different age groups–toddlers, school age, teenagers, adults.
- At what age do responsibilities begin? End?
- Do people respond to responsibilities the same way?
- Do roles and responsibilities change with age? Environment? Circumstances?
- Do you enjoy all of your roles?
- How responsible are you?

What to do:

- Ask students what they think the terms "role" and "responsibility" mean. List responses on the board. Students can use these to refer to when answering Question 1.
- Read and discuss the paragraph about personal roles with the whole class. Ask several students to define their roles so all students will gain a clear understanding of what is required in Question 2. Remind them to think of what they do at home, at school, in clubs and teams, or in the community.
- Students will probably provide more honest responses to Questions 2 – 5 if working independently. Discuss what is involved in each question, then assist as required.
- Those students who wish to could share responses with the class.

Answers:

Teacher check

Additional Activities

- In small groups, rehearse then role-play certain roles, showing irresponsible and responsible behaviors for each. Discuss what each performance is trying to show.
- As a class, devise a checklist of how to be a responsible person.
- Use characters in novels to discuss their roles and how responsible or irresponsible they were.

Background Information

A person's "role" is the expected or usual part played in life. People have different roles. For example, a teacher has a professional role at school and roles at home as possibly a wife/husband/partner or parent. A responsibility is a duty of care. Within each role, a person has certain responsibilities to perform. Roles and responsibilities change with age and environment.

Roles and responsibilities help to shape a person's character. It is important that children are given responsibilities for this reason. These will:

- *provide them with chances to show their knowledge, skills and understanding of what is required.*

- *develop their self-worth, provide a reason for doing something and encourage commitment to keep going.*

People do not all respond in the same way to responsibilities. Shy, less confident people may not enjoy or take on leadership roles in a group, but may work well within a group and still be responsible.

Others may act irresponsibly and cannot be relied upon. Some people are more responsible in some roles than others.

What do you think the words "role" and "responsibility" mean?

1 Use keywords and phrases to explain each word.

Role	Responsibility

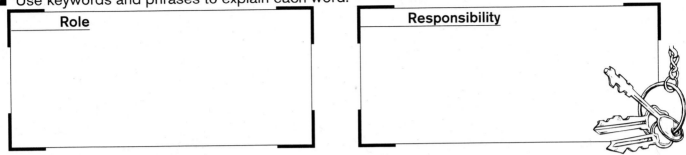

People have more than one role, especially as they get older.
Your roles might include being a student in your class, a member of a club or team, a son or daughter, and a brother or sister. Your roles are at school, home and in the community.
You have certain responsibilities within each role.

2 Choose up to six of your roles and explain your responsibilities for each.
Give yourself a mark out of 10 for how well you carry out each role (10 being the best.).

Role	Responsibility	Rating

3 Now consider how responsible you are overall. Rate yourself (10 being the most responsible).

1	2	3	4	5	6	7	8	9	10

4 (a) What role are you best at?

_____

(b) Why do you think this is?

_____

_____

_____

5 Could you improve the way you behave in certain roles?

yes   no

Explain.

_____

_____

_____

Indicator

• Recognizes personal feelings related to given statements.

The Lesson

Discussion points:

• How well do you know yourself?
• Do you think you have good self-esteem?
• How do you think you would react in an emergency?
• Do you like talking about yourself?

What to do:

• Use the worksheet as a one-to-one conference, a portfolio activity, or as a teacher record.

Answers:

Answers will vary

Additional Activities

• Students complete a "report card" about themselves, giving themselves a score out of 10 on areas such as attitude, decision making, effort, confidence and other similar attributes.

• Students complete the report card with a personal comment on how they can improve their scores in the above areas. They write themselves an achievable goal.

Background Information

Body language such as facial expressions, stance and posture are keys to knowing how a person is feeling. Different situations evoke different emotions. Students should be aware that each of us may react to different situations in different ways. Students need to learn to show feelings in ways that are helpful to them and others, and not in ways that are hurtful.

My Thoughts and Feelings

Answer yes or no.	Yes	No
1. I eat a well-balanced diet.		
2. I like setting goals and achieving them.		
3. I get along with my peers well.		
4. I always wear a helmet when I'm riding my bike.		
5. I like new challenges.		
6. I enjoy being physically active.		
7. I prefer quieter, less active activities.		
8. I could improve my diet.		
9. I get plenty of sleep.		
10. I find it easy to make friends.		
11. I am confident in speaking my opinions.		
12. I am a good team member.		
13. I feel shy in speaking out.		
14. I find it hard to get to sleep.		
15. I do not mind being alone sometimes.		
16. I like my appearance.		
17. I should exercise more.		
18. I have lots of interests.		
19. I wish I looked different.		
20. My friends influence what I do.		
21. I know how to respond to unsafe situations.		
22. I am a positive person.		
23. I am able to find enough time to relax.		
24. I'm comfortable with the changes of puberty.		
25. I always take responsibility for my actions.		
26. I experience some conflict with my family.		
27. I'm confident of resisting any pressure to use drugs.		
28. I am able to set goals to improve my lifestyle.		
29. I use community facilities to keep fit.		
30. I'm confident I can recognize an emergency situation and deal with it.		
31. I cope well with peer pressure.		
32. I'm able to select foods that are good for me when I make my own choices.		
33. I enjoy including a variety of different foods in my diet.		
34. I understand that the media may not always promote things realistically.		
35. I'm able to make decisions with confidence.		
36. I have a positive body image.		
37. Close relationships are important to me.		
38. My parents influence a lot of what I am able to do.		
39. I'm an emotional type of person.		
40. I enjoy getting up each morning.		

Indicator

- Recognizes personal feelings related to given statements.

The Lesson

Discussion points:

- How well do you know yourself?
- Do you think you have good self-esteem?
- How do you think you would react in an emergency?
- Do you like talking about yourself?
- Do you ever make personal goals for yourself?

What to do:

- Use the worksheet as a one-to-one conference, a portfolio activity, or as a teacher record.

Answers:

Answers will vary

Additional Activities

- Imagine you have suddenly become famous. A magazine has asked for a "personal profile" all about you. They would like to know what you are like, what you enjoy doing and what you value. Write your own personal profile. Write it in the third person (he, she, etc.) and add a picture.

Background Information

The way we feel about ourselves has a major effect on our lives and our relationships with others, in terms of decisions we make and how we treat ourselves and others.

The way we feel about ourselves is called self-esteem. When we generally feel good about ourselves, we say we have high self-esteem; when we generally feel poorly about ourselves, we say we have low self-esteem. People with high self-esteem feel:

- *happy.*
- *okay as a person.*
- *a strong belief in themselves.*
- *they have a good future to look forward to.*
- *enjoyment toward the world.*
- *energetic and hopeful.*
- *confident in the ability to be able to change things.*
- *comfortable enough to join in with others.*
- *happy with every success—even if it is small.*
- *capable of looking for different ways to succeed.*
- *positive enough to encourage others.*
- *respect for differences they see in others.*

When we have high self-esteem, we don't have to boast or try to prove how good we are to other people. We just need to believe in ourselves and what we think we can do.

Answer yes or no.

1.	I am enjoying school this year.	Yes	No
2.	I am pleased with the results I get.	Yes	No
3.	I get along with my classmates well.	Yes	No
4.	I feel confident with the work we do.	Yes	No
5.	I am a responsible class member.	Yes	No
6.	I always finish assigned homework.	Yes	No
7.	I feel as though I am a valuable class member.	Yes	No
8.	I set high standards for myself.	Yes	No
9.	I am able to concentrate well on my work.	Yes	No
10.	I find it easy to learn something new.	Yes	No
11.	I feel as though I can handle most problems I face at school.	Yes	No
12.	I am involved in many after-school activities.	Yes	No
13.	I have good ideas.	Yes	No
14.	It is hard for me to make new friends.	Yes	No
15.	I am a happy person.	Yes	No
16.	I can get bored easily.	Yes	No
17.	My parents have high expectations of me.	Yes	No
18.	I love being faced with new challenges.	Yes	No
19.	I often want things my own way.	Yes	No
20.	Sometimes I wish I were a different person.	Yes	No
21.	My peers respect me.	Yes	No
22.	I lead a well-balanced lifestyle.	Yes	No
23.	My friends are interested in my opinions.	Yes	No
24.	I can be easily influenced by my peers.	Yes	No
25.	I often run out of time and don't get things finished.	Yes	No
26.	I am able to set goals and work towards achieving them.	Yes	No
27.	I am a good communicator.	Yes	No
28.	I have a positive attitude.	Yes	No
29.	I have some trouble handling conflict situations.	Yes	No
30.	I am able to work well with others.	Yes	No
31.	I have healthy eating habits.	Yes	No
32.	I always get enough sleep.	Yes	No
33.	Sometimes I worry about the way I look.	Yes	No
34.	I have a good relationship with my parents.	Yes	No
35.	I make an effort to always try my best.	Yes	No
36.	I exercise on a regular basis.	Yes	No
37.	I feel confident and informed about the changes during puberty.	Yes	No

Indicator

- Considers the importance of self-worth.

The Lesson

Discussion points:

- What do you like about yourself?
- What are some things about yourself you think you need to work on or improve?
- What is your greatest achievement?
- What personal qualities do you admire in others?
- How do other people make you feel special and important?
- What makes you feel as though you are not special and important?
- Why is it important to feel good about yourself?

What to do:

- With the students' help, define "personal qualities." The definition decided upon should indicate they are features of a person's nature.
- Ask the students to suggest qualities they admire in other people and list them on the board. You may choose to use a stimulus for this activity, such as reading a short story and asking the students to identify the positive qualities of the main character. Alternatively, you could start the list with your own suggestions. Some personal qualities that may be suggested are empathy, honesty, helpfulness, determination and trustworthiness.
- Ask the students to suggest skills they admire in other people and list them on the chalkboard; for example: having skills in music, art, or sports; being a good listener, speaker, or mediator.
- Ask the students to complete the worksheet. They could look at the chalkboard if they are having trouble thinking of ideas.
- When the worksheet is completed, the students could write their answers to Question 3 again on separate sheets of paper. The sheets of paper could be shuffled and given out to the class. Each student could then read out the answer he/she has been given. The class could vote on the five answers they think would win the competition. Finally, the students who wrote the answers could identify themselves.

Answers:

Answers will vary

Additional Activities

- Discuss how certain personal qualities and/or skills could be developed or worked on.
- Students could draw their favorite symbol from Question 2 on a sheet of poster board, with a brief description and their name. The symbols could be displayed in the classroom.

Background Information

The ability to feel comfortable about yourself—to feel you are a worthwhile person—is an important step in growing up. Children need to feel worthwhile and important. They also need to be able to like and accept themselves so they can like and accept others.

Everybody is important and unique–including you!
When you are feeling bad, it is easy to forget about all the good qualities and skills you have.
Sometimes you need to remind yourself of how special you are so you can feel good about yourself again. When you feel this way, it is easier to get along with others and enjoy life.

1 Ask a friend to list five words or phrases that describe what he/she likes about you. Add at least three things you like about yourself.

Friend's list

- _____
- _____
- _____
- _____
- _____

My list

- _____
- _____
- _____

2 Draw symbols that show three things you do well or have achieved in; for example, if you are good at music, you could draw a musical note. Write a label underneath each symbol.

3 Imagine your school is looking for a small group of students from your grade to represent it at a festival. You are eager to be chosen. Use the ideas on this page to help you complete the entry form.

 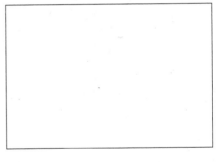

FUN FESTIVAL!

If you would like to be a part of the Fun Festival, please complete the statement below in **2⁵** words or less. You should describe your best qualities and any skills or abilities you have. Good luck!

I think I would make a good school representative because

_____

_____

_____

Indicators

- Shows an understanding of self-esteem.
- Considers some ways self-esteem is influenced.

The Lesson

Discussion points:

- What makes you feel good about yourself? What makes you feel bad about yourself? Discuss which things are in the students' control to change for the better.
- What type of body language might people with low self-esteem show?
- What type of body language might people with high self-esteem show?
- What are the positive effects of having high self-esteem?
- Discuss people the students know who generally seem to have high self-esteem. Why do you think this is?
- Is it possible for your self-esteem to be too high? Discuss.

What to do:

- Read aloud the text at the top of the page. Discuss the term "self-esteem" to ensure that all students have understood its meaning.
- Questions 1 and 2 could be completed in small groups. Encourage discussion. The answers could be reported back to the class.
- Before students work on Question 3, a class discussion could be held in which possible scenarios and endings are suggested. Encourage students to use appropriate body language during their role-plays to show how the characters are feeling.

Answers:

Teacher check

Additional Activities

- Ask students to write scripts for their role-plays.
- After watching movies or television programs, discuss the self-esteem of the main characters and how it affected the plot.

Background Information

A healthy self-esteem can be encouraged in the classroom through drama games, praise, encouraging empathy among students and supporting the school bullying policy. Students are often bullied because they have low self-esteem.

How you feel about yourself is sometimes called your self-esteem.
If you are feeling good about yourself, we say you have high self-esteem.
If you are feeling bad about yourself, we say you have low self-esteem.
Some people manage to have high self-esteem most of the time.
If they find themselves in situations that make their self-esteem drop, they do things that make it soar!

Many things can cause your self-esteem to drop. These include:

- *being bullied.*
- *hearing or thinking negative things about yourself.*
- *making mistakes.*
- *not reaching a goal.*

There are also many things that can cause your self-esteem to soar. These include:

- *having positive friends.*
- *hearing or thinking good things about yourself.*
- *helping others.*
- *reaching a goal.*

1 For each of the situations below, mark if someone's self-esteem is likely to drop or soar.

(a) Receiving a certificate for working hard in English.

| **drop** | **soar** |

(b) Being called names.

| **drop** | **soar** |

(c) Receiving a compliment.

| **drop** | **soar** |

(d) Being bullied by an older child.

| **drop** | **soar** |

2 Choose one of the situations that you decided would make someone's self-esteem drop. Suggest ideas that might make that person feel better again.

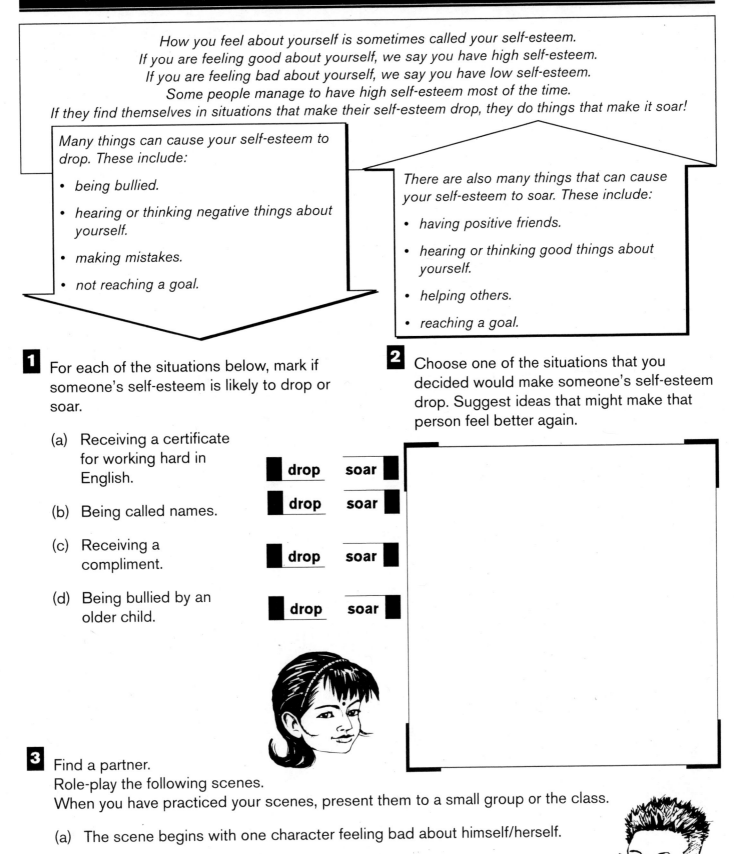

3 Find a partner.
Role-play the following scenes.
When you have practiced your scenes, present them to a small group or the class.

(a) The scene begins with one character feeling bad about himself/herself.

(b) The scene begins with one character feeling good about himself/herself.

Each scene should have a positive ending.

Indicators

- Identifies strengths and weaknesses.
- Identifies steps to achieve a goal.
- Writes phrases to provide encouragement towards achieving a goal.

The Lesson

Discussion points:

- What are "strengths" and "weaknesses"?
- What are your strengths and weaknesses?
- How do you feel when you achieve a goal?
- How do you feel knowing you are good at something?
- How do you feel when you fail at something?
- What do you do? Do you give in and never attempt that activity again?
- Do you keep on trying until you get better?
- Do you set goals to achieve success?

What to do:

- Discuss the questions above.
- Allow students to read the introduction and begin Question 1. Students should be given this time to ask questions if they aren't sure of something.
- Students read the italicized print after Question 1 and answer Question 2.
- Students read Question 3 and complete their answers.
- Students read the italicized print and complete their answer for Question 4.
- You may collect the work and mark later.

Answers:

Answers will vary as all responses are individual.

Additional Activities

- Students make a list of achievements for the past year.
- Practice setting goals, whether academic, sporting, or personal.
- Students list good characteristics of well-known people such as TV personalities and sports stars whom they would like to emulate.
- Students discuss or list occasions when they have failed to do something. Find positive aspects of failure, such as trying harder or selecting different goals.
- With a partner or small group, role-play a scenario where success was achieved.
- Create a chart of positive "talk" to encourage each other towards a goal.

Background Information

As unique, valuable individuals, we all have our strengths and weaknesses. It is important to be pleased with our successes as well as the manner in which we handle failure. This is difficult for adults to cope with as well as children. Risk taking can be very difficult, but children should be praised and rewarded for any attempts to try something new as well as for gaining success. By setting goals and small steps to reach them, students are able to experience small successes, motivating them to continue. It is often necessary to attempt a new task or skill many times before succeeding. In this way valuable knowledge, skills and values will be learned.

©World Teachers Press®

Everyone has things they do well and things they are not so good at.

1 Fill one side with a list of things you are good at and the other with a list of things you are not so good. Remember to include things such as being a good friend and being useful at home.

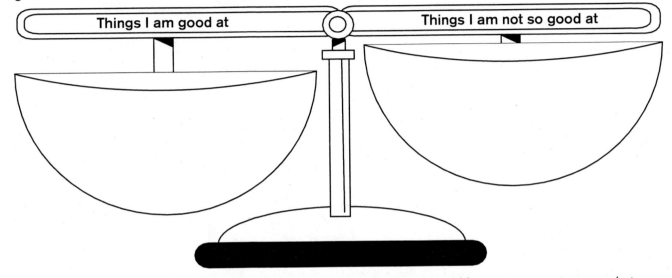

| Things I am good at | Things I am not so good at |

We can feel better about ourselves when we try to improve those things we are not so good at, whether we succeed or not. Trying is the important thing.

2 Choose something you are not very good at and write a plan showing the steps to improve.

I am not very good at:

_____

I can improve by:

- _____

- _____

- _____

- _____

3 Write some "good things" to say to encourage yourself towards your goals. An example is given for you.

"It takes a long time, but I will achieve little steps until I reach my goal."

_____

_____

_____

_____

Sometimes our goals and dreams may seem unattainable.

4 Write something that you would really love to do when you are older.

_____

_____

Other people have achieved the seemingly impossible, so make a plan and **GO FOR IT!!!**

Indicators

- Selects strategies to develop self-esteem.
- Writes positive statements or words about himself/herself.
- Compares descriptions about himself/herself.

The Lesson

Discussion points:

- Why do we need to feel good about ourselves?
- What does a confident person look like?
- What things offend you?
- Why shouldn't we criticize others?
- Why is it good to say how we feel?
- Why isn't it good to dwell on bad things that happened in the past?

What to do:

- Discuss the questions above.
- Read the list of things which encourage low self-esteem and discuss them. Students complete Questions 2 and 3.
- A friend should complete the first box in Question 4, then return the worksheet to the owner for him/her to complete the second box. The student then compares the two lists.

Answers:

1. Answers will vary
2. Answers will vary, but may include the following:
   (a) Make a decision and stick to it. If it is the wrong one, so what? We all make mistakes, but we learn from them.
   (b) Ignore other people when they say something bad. No-one is perfect! Tell yourself some good things about yourself.
   (c) Try not to say many bad things about yourself or others. "If you can't say something nice, then say nothing!"
   (d) Say how you feel if someone upsets you. This will develop communication and relieve tension.
   (e) Forget what has happened before. You can't change the past! Each day can be a new beginning. Be positive and start afresh.

3. – 4. Answers will vary

Additional Activities

- Role-play standing tall and walking confidently.
- Encourage "assertive" behavior rather than aggressive behavior.
- Practice saying "I" statements to express feelings and what you would like to happen.
- Practice saying positive things about someone or something.
- Compile a list or chart for each student using positive words or sentences. Read it each day.

Background Information

Self-esteem can be encouraged in the classroom through drama games, praise and encouraging empathy among students. Students can talk to each other in a positive manner, have positive friends, set small goals and aim to reach them, show positive body language (such as standing up straight without arms folded in front), and help others.

It is important that the students are aware of the need to:

- *Say positive things to themselves.*
- *Think positive things about themselves.*
- *Learn to accept that someone may look better than them, is thinner, or has nicer hair today. Their only concern is themselves and no one else. Developing self-esteem is a long-term process. Always aim to encourage and give praise when it is due.*

> Self-esteem deals with how we feel about ourselves. If you feel confident and good about yourself, we say you have high self-esteem. If you feel bad about yourself and have no confidence, we say you have low self-esteem.

1 Read this list of habits which encourage low self-esteem.

(a) Doubt yourself constantly.

(b) Take offense easily.

(c) Criticize yourself and others.

(d) Keep your feelings to yourself.

(e) Keep thinking about the bad things that have happened to you.

2 Write a strategy to counteract each of the habits from Question 1.

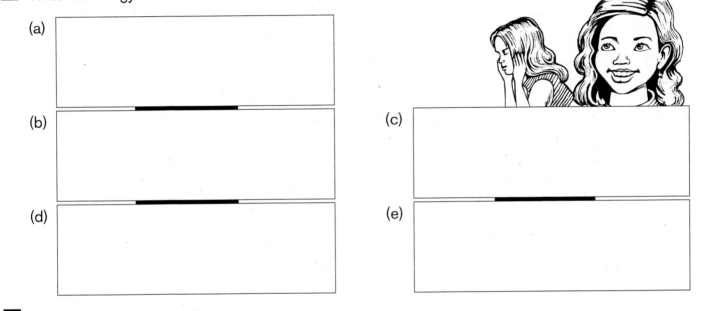

(a)

(b)

(c)

(d)

(e)

3 Complete the statements below using positive thoughts.

(a) "I am important because _____

_____

_____

_____ "

(b) "I am a good friend because _____

_____

_____ "

4 Ask a friend to write positive words about you in the first box, then complete the second yourself. Compare them when you have finished.

My friend's list

My list

Indicators

- Identifies strategies to improve his/her own self-esteem.
- Uses "I" statements to demonstrate positive self-worth.
- Demonstrates possible situations in which he/she could take a risk.

The Lesson

Discussion points:

- What is self-esteem?
- Why is high self-esteem so important?
- Is there a difference between high self-esteem and being smug or conceited? Explain.
- Where does high self-esteem come from?
- What causes low self-esteem?
- Can we sometimes be too critical of ourselves?

What to do:

- Use the Discussion points above as a warm-up to the lesson. One possible approach to the discussion is to write each Discussion point on a piece of card stock. Organize the class into groups of five or six and ensure each group has a set of discussion cards.
- Give the groups five minutes to discuss each point. After each Discussion point, select one student to report the main points of his/her group's discussion to the whole class.
- Ensure a safe and supportive environment is available to students when sharing their personal views. This means each student is allowed to speak uninterrupted and other students are to use active listening skills without the use of "put-downs."
- Sit students in a large circle. Start with yourself and use an "I" statement to state something you are good at or enjoy or a positive trait; e.g., "I am a really helpful person, I enjoy helping others wherever I can." Take turns around the circle so each student can make an "I" statement. If a student has difficulty, other students may offer suggestions, but the student must complete the "I" statement.
- Students can then complete Questions 1 and 2 on the worksheet.
- Read through the text provided on the worksheet relating to risk taking. Share and discuss some examples with students in regard to issues that may be holding him/her back from taking risks, and discuss in depth risks that are too dangerous to contemplate.
- Students can then complete the remaining activities on the worksheet.

Answers:

1. positive, self-belief, energetic, capable, happy, successful, hopeful, confident, tolerant, dignity, self-worth, assertive, secure, achieve, loved
2. – 4. Answers will vary

Additional Activities

- Encourage students to set a risk-taking goal. Plan the approach and consider both positive and negative consequences. Set a date by which he/she hopes to have achieved the goal.
- Each student needs to think about the person he/she wishes to be and how he/she would like things to be in his/her life. How can he/she make it happen?

Background Information

The way we feel about ourselves has a major effect on our lives and our relationships with others, in terms of decisions we make, and how we treat ourselves and others.

The way we feel about ourselves is called self-esteem. When we generally feel good about ourselves, we say we have high self-esteem; when we generally feel poorly about ourselves, we say we have low self-esteem. People with high self-esteem feel:

- *happy.*
- *okay as a person.*
- *a strong belief in themselves.*
- *they have a good future to look forward to.*
- *enjoyment toward the world.*
- *energetic and hopeful.*
- *confident in the ability to be able to change things.*
- *comfortable enough to join in with others.*
- *happy with every success—even if it is small.*
- *capable of looking for different ways to succeed.*
- *positive enough to encourage others.*
- *they can respect differences they see in others.*

When we have high self-esteem we don't have to boast or try to prove how good we are to other people. We just need to believe in ourselves and what we think we can do.

1 Find 15 words in the wordsearch that are related to good self-esteem.

p	o	s	i	t	i	v	e	a	m	k	a
s	t	n	e	d	i	f	n	o	c	v	j
f	e	s	e	l	f	w	o	r	t	h	s
a	q	c	g	t	f	l	h	b	e	n	u
s	y	e	u	a	a	b	u	n	g	t	c
s	p	r	f	r	d	k	e	i	w	n	c
e	p	s	h	e	e	r	c	l	b	a	e
r	a	e	v	i	g	j	d	o	i	r	s
t	h	o	p	e	f	u	l	x	p	e	s
i	l	y	t	i	n	g	i	d	c	l	f
v	z	i	e	v	e	i	h	c	a	o	u
e	c	a	p	a	b	l	e	y	d	t	l

2 List four ways you could improve your self-esteem.

(a) _____

(b) _____

(c) _____

(d) _____

Those people with a healthy self-esteem often find it easier to take risks and move out of their comfort zone. This means they are able to experience new things without worrying about what may happen if they are not successful. Many people are reluctant to try new things or push themselves a little further to see what they are capable of achieving.

3 Give four reasons why you may be reluctant to take risks.

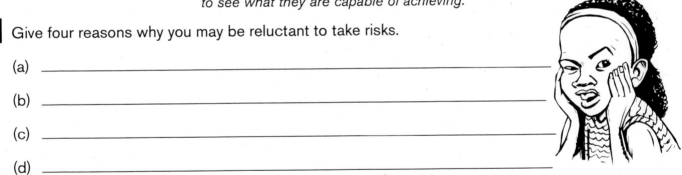

(a) _____

(b) _____

(c) _____

(d) _____

Some risks are dangerous and some are just plain stupid! Contemplating any such risks requires you to think long and hard about the consequences. Can you harm yourself or cause someone else grief? Will your actions break the law?

Risks I would love to take ... one day!	**Risks I would never bother with!**

Indicators

- Identifies how he/she responds to different situations.
- Discusses and practices possible responses to different situations.
- Uses "I" statements with confidence to demonstrate assertive behavior.

The Lesson

Discussion points:

- How might you act if you are acting in a passive manner?
- How might you act if you are acting in an aggressive manner?
- How might you act if you are acting in an assertive manner?
- What are "I" statements?
- What are the steps you might take to learn how to be assertive?
- What are the benefits of being assertive?

What to do:

- Discuss the first three discussion points and encourage students to provide real-life examples of each type of behavior. Discuss how the person who is "dealing out" the behavior and the person "receiving" the behavior might feel in each situation.
- Discuss the fourth discussion point.
- Practice making "I" statements. You can either provide various situations for the students to give an "I" statement for, or they can think of a situation in which an "I" statement could be used. Sit students in a large circle. Start with yourself and use an "I" statement to state how you feel about a situation; e.g., "I feel annoyed when my roommate doesn't do the dishes because it seems as though she takes advantage of me. I would like her to take turns washing the dishes." Take turns around the circle so each student can make an "I" statement. If a student has difficulty, other students may offer suggestions, but the student must complete the "I" statement.
- Complete Questions 1 and 2 on the worksheet. Discuss student responses to the activities.
- Discuss the final two discussion points above, then direct students to consider and complete Questions 3 and 4 on the worksheet.

Answers:

Answers will vary

Additional Activities

- Role-play various situations to allow students the opportunity to practice being assertive. Encourage students to look at body language, posture, voice control, eye contact and the use of "I" statements.
- Make a list of attributes a passive person, assertive person and an aggressive person may have. These could be written in a full-size outline of a person and displayed on the wall as a reference for students. Students can then use the posters to check themselves and how they are reacting to a situation.
- Students could have a forum to discuss any situations that are occurring which bother them. Other students could offer suggestions to help solve the problem in an assertive manner. Remember, anything discussed at these forums remains confidential and students who are not able to honor this should not be involved.

Background Information

There are three ways to respond to different situations:

- *Passive—acting as though the rights of others are more important than his/hers.*
- *Aggressive—acting as though his/her rights are more important than others.*
- *Assertive—respecting others and himself/herself equally.*

Developing assertive behavior is essential to developing positive self-esteem. To be assertive, one must have a level of confidence to be able to communicate one's needs, wants and feelings without hurting others.

When communicating in an assertive manner, people are:

- *being honest without being rude or hurtful.*
- *considering what they really want to achieve.*
- *allowing others to feel safe and get what they want too.*
- *respecting themselves and others too.*
- *not intentionally hurting others.*

The use of "I" statements rather than "you" statements is an important part of being assertive; for example, "I don't like what you are saying to me and I want you to stop it now!" rather than "You always tease me."

Students also need to be encouraged to look confident when practicing assertive behavior. It can make all the difference.

1 How do you normally respond to different situations?
Circle the approach you use or color the circles if you have a mix of two approaches.

○—○—○—○—○—○—○—◯—○—○—○—○—○—○—◯

passive   assertive   aggressive

2 Write an assertive, aggressive and passive response to each of the following.
Remember, when being assertive, "I" statements are very helpful.

Situation	Assertive response	Aggressive response	Passive response
Your parents refuse to let you stay over at your friend's house on a weekend night.			
A friend shares a personal secret of yours with someone else.			
Your mom wants to make your graduation outfit, but you have your heart set on something in a store.			
A class member refuses to cooperate during a group project.			

3 List some of the positive effects assertive behavior might have in your life.

_____

_____

_____

_____

4 Write a sentence explaining how you will endeavor to use assertive behavior in the future.

_____

_____

Indicators

- Generates personal goals which are based on being fit and active.
- Devises strategies to attain his/her personal goals.
- Evaluates his/her decisions in the process of setting personal goals.

The Lesson

Discussion points:

- What is a goal?
- Do you ever set goals for yourself?
- Do you always achieve your goals?
- How do you feel when you achieve your goals? How do you feel when you don't achieve your goals?
- What is your definition of success?
- "It is okay to set lower goals than to risk failure by setting higher ones." Agree or disagree?

Materials needed/Preparation:

- Organize students into groups of five or six.

What to do:

- Begin by discussing the first question from the Discussion points in groups. Students then report their ideas about what a goal is to the class.
- Direct students to the worksheet and read through the Steps for Goal Setting. Talk about each point and ask students to contribute their own examples of goal setting.
- Discuss questions two and three from the Discussion points in small groups. Spend a short period of time with each group to gather an idea of who sets goals and who doesn't. As a whole class, talk about the importance of setting goals in order to be successful (see Background Information).
- As a class, brainstorm some goals students may like to set; for example, in health and fitness, the arts or spelling, developing new friendships, or being more organized. Remember it must be expressed in terms which can be measured. Establish which goals would be long-term or short-term.
- Discuss questions four and five from the Discussion points. Record students' answers on the board using keywords and phrases. Develop a class definition for success. This could be presented on a chart and used to motivate students on a daily basis.
- Direct students to complete the table in Question 1 on the worksheet. Encourage students to select one short-term and one long-term goal.
- Discuss or debate the final statement from the Discussion points in small groups.
- Each student can then complete Question 2 by evaluating his/her decisions and modify his/her goals as required.

Answers:

Answers will vary

Additional Activities

- Students can periodically check their goals to ensure they are on target for meeting them.
- Set some class goals that will encourage students to work together for a common purpose.
- Practice setting short-term and long-term goals on a regular basis. Evaluate students' success rates.
- Present the class's definition of "success" on a large, bright chart as a motivational tool.
- Display class goals on a large chart near the "success" chart in order to keep the class on target.

Background Information

People who experience success set goals. They formulate their goals and set into motion a strategy to help them meet their goal within a set time. Those who are successful often have a mentor they report to on a regular basis who helps to keep them on track. Successful people:

- *have a clear vision of what they want and where they wish to be in life.*
- *develop a clear strategy which states how, when and what they need to do.*
- *experience passion for their goal. They are excited about it!*
- *are honest with themselves about what they need to do and about their strengths and weaknesses.*
- *are flexible.*
- *take risks or move outside the area where they feel most comfortable.*
- *surround themselves with people who want them to be successful.*
- *put goals into action and achieve them.*
- *prioritize goals and actions that need to be achieved.*
- *manage their own mental, physical, emotional and spiritual self.*

Setting Goals

Steps for Goal Setting

1. What is your goal?   *Write it clearly.*
2. When do you want to achieve your goal?   *Set a target date.*
3. How will you work toward achieving your goal?   *Plan a step-by-step strategy.*
4. Who will help you achieve your goal?   *Arrange to have a mentor.*
5. Why is this goal so important to you?   *Consider why you want to achieve it.*

1 Set yourself two goals.

	Goal 1	Goal 2
Goal		
Target date		
Strategy		
Possible obstacles		
Mentor		
How will I know when I have achieved my goal?		
This goal is important to me because …		

2 Evaluate your decisions in setting your personal goals.

(a) I set realistic goals.   Yes | No

(b) I set realistic time lines.   Yes | No

(c) My strategies are clearly laid out for me to follow.   Yes | No

(d) I have included approaches to solve any problems that may occur.   Yes | No

(e) I have selected a mentor whom I trust to help me.   Yes | No

Indicators

- Generates personal goals which are based on being fit and active.
- Devises strategies to attain his/her personal goals.
- Evaluates his/her decisions in the process of setting personal goals.

The Lesson

Discussion points:

- What is a goal?
- Do you ever set goals for yourself?
- Do you always achieve your goals?
- How do you feel when you achieve your goals? How do you feel when you don't achieve your goals?
- What is your definition of success?
- "It is okay to set lower goals than to risk failure by setting higher ones." Agree or disagree?

What to do:

- Discuss the first point above. Include in the discussion the difference between short-term and long-term goals. Read the Background Information to the students.
- Discuss the second point above. Incorporate the concept of prioritizing goals and setting target dates to achieve them.
- Discuss the third point above. Encourage students to evaluate the reasons they might not achieve a set goal. Discuss how obstacles can be overcome and develop a list of strategies which may assist in achieving goals. Lead into the fourth point from the discussion points above.
- Brainstorm the fifth point as a whole class; develop a sentence which sums up the class's idea of success. Display in a prominent location.
- Discuss the final point. Talk about the advantages and disadvantages of stepping outside the "comfort zone" or staying inside the "comfort zone."
- Students can then complete the worksheet. Encourage students to take time and give thought and consideration to the goals recorded on the worksheet. "What is most important to you in the area of ... (school, health and fitness, family, and home life)?"
- Students follow through with their goals. Periodically, follow-up with students to evaluate progress toward achieving stated goals.

Answers:

Answers will vary

Additional Activities

- Set some class goals to encourage students to work together for a common purpose.
- Students can also set themselves goals in other areas, such as personal development, an out-of-school interest, an environmental project, volunteer work, a hobby, etc.
- Develop a school goal, break it down into small, achievable stages, and work towards achieving the goal.

Background Information

People who experience success set goals. They formulate their goals and set into motion a strategy to help them meet their goals within a set time. Those who are successful often have a mentor they report to on a regular basis who helps to keep them on track. Successful people:

- *have a clear vision of what they want and where they wish to be in life.*
- *develop a clear strategy that states how, when and what they need to do.*
- *experience passion about their goal. They are excited about it!*
- *are honest with themselves about what they need to do, and about their strengths and weaknesses.*
- *are flexible.*
- *take a risk, move outside the area where they feel most comfortable.*
- *surround themselves with people who want them to be successful.*
- *put a plan into action and get it done.*
- *prioritize goals and actions that need to be done.*
- *manage their own mental, physical, emotional and spiritual well-being.*

1 Set a goal related to school. Think about what is important to you!

Goal: _____

Why it is important to me: _____

_____

Target date: _____ Achieved: _____ Steps to take to achieve my goal:

Immediate action (daily or weekly)	**Short-term** (weekly or monthly)	**Long-term** (monthly or longer)

2 Set a goal related to health and fitness. Think about what is important to you!

Goal: _____

Why it is important to me: _____

_____

Target date: _____ Achieved: _____ Steps to take to achieve my goal:

Immediate action (daily or weekly)	**Short-term** (weekly or monthly)	**Long-term** (monthly or longer)

3 Set a goal related to family and home life. Think about what is important to you!

Goal: _____

Why it is important to me: _____

_____

Target date: _____ Achieved: _____ Steps to take to achieve my goal:

Immediate action (daily or weekly)	**Short-term** (weekly or monthly)	**Long-term** (monthly or longer)

Indicators

- Identifies events that cause stress.
- Identifies activities that aid relaxation.
- Completes an action plan to combat stress.
- Completes a simple time management format.

The Lesson

Discussion points:

- What stresses you out?
- What makes you feel relaxed and good about yourself?
- How does feeling good about yourself affect your day?
- How do you cope with everyday situations?
- What are your favorite forms of exercise?
- What forms of music relax you?
- Are there particular places that make you feel relaxed?

What to do:

- Discuss the points listed above. Students read the opening paragraph and complete Question 1.
- Read Question 2 to emphasize the steps. Discuss these to make sure that students fully understand them. Students complete Questions 2 and 3 independently. Students may assist you in creating a timetable of daily class events on the board, showing times and learning areas covered, play times, etc. Compare the amount of time spent completing lessons to that for relaxation.
- Read Question 4 to the students and allow them to attempt a time management strategy for the time after school until bedtime.

Answers:

Answers will vary since all responses are individual.

Additional Activities

- Use favorite raps or rhymes as a short relaxation period between lessons. Make students aware of these times.
- Incorporate stretching or movement exercises to relieve stress during the day.
- Play soothing background music while the students are working quietly. Allow students to bring in appropriate choices.
- Encourage the use of a daily diary to reinforce time management skills.
- Reward good use of work time with extra free time.

Background Information

Mental or emotional health is as important to maintain as physical health. Good mental health involves:

- *feeling good about yourself and your life.*
- *being able to respond constructively to stress in your life.*
- *being able to cope with events that occur in your life.*
- *self-esteem or confidence.*
- *how you see yourself and the future.*

When you feel stressed or worried, physical reactions occur, including a fast heartbeat, tense muscles, a tight stomach, feeling sick, fast breathing, sweating, difficulty sleeping, or waking up still feeling tired. There are many ways to build positive mental health, including doing things that you are good at and enjoy, developing personal skills to help when dealing with people, investigating new ways to cope with everyday problems, getting involved with clubs, committees, causes, helping others, or occasionally taking risks and trying new things, having fun and enjoying yourself.

At times, you may feel like everything in your life seems to be going wrong and you can't cope.
You may feel tired, grumpy, anxious, or confused.
During these times it is difficult to think clearly and to concentrate.
There are strategies to deal with stress to help you get back on track.

1 Complete the boxes.

I feel stressed when ...	I relax by ...

2 When you feel stressed, you should:

- *Think about what it is that is worrying you.*

- *Talk to someone you trust about your problem.*

- *Don't agree to do any extra tasks if you really don't want to.*

- *Learn to relax.*

3 Complete the steps below to create an action plan to help you deal with stress. Use the steps from Question 2.

• I am stressed because _____

_____

_____

• I will talk to _____ because

_____

_____

• I won't be able to _____

because _____

_____

_____

• I will relax by _____

_____

4 It is easier to cope with stress if your time is managed sensibly. On a separate sheet of paper:

- Write a list of tasks that MUST be done (such as homework or projects).
- Write a list of what you would LIKE to do.
- Place the "MUST-DO" tasks in order of importance (or what needs to be done first).
- Work out the time needed to complete them. (Note: These have to be done properly!)
- Do a little bit each day to make the tasks manageable.
- Place some "LIKE-TO-DO" activities every so often on the list to provide some relief.

NOTE: It is better to get the MUST-DO tasks done first, to give you more time for LIKE-TO-DO things.

Indicators

- Understands some ways in which stress can be managed.
- Considers how he/she deals with stress.

The Lesson

Discussion points:

- Which situations cause you the most stress? Have these changed as you have grown older?
- What are some common ways people show stress?
- How could you help someone who is stressed?
- Discuss the importance of relaxing and "chilling out."
- Discuss the effects of poorly managed stress; e.g., anxiety, drug abuse, withdrawal, aggression, or illness.

What to do:

- You may prefer the students to work individually for Question 4.
- After students have reported their answers to Question 4, a class or small-group discussion should follow.

Answers:

Answers will vary

Additional Activities

- Brainstorm other suggestions for ways students can avoid or deal with stress.
- Brainstorm common causes of stress for teenagers and adults.
- Collect newspaper or magazine articles which discuss aspects of stress. Students can write comments about the ideas in the articles.

Display Ideas

- Display a list of ways students in the class relax.

Background Information

Mental or emotional health is as important to maintain as physical health. Good mental health involves:

- *feeling good about yourself and your life.*
- *being able to respond constructively to stress in your life.*
- *being able to cope with events that occur in your life.*
- *self-esteem or confidence.*
- *how you see yourself and the future.*

When you feel stressed or worried, physical reactions occur, including fast heartbeat, tense muscles, "tight" stomach or feeling sick, fast breathing, sweating, difficulty sleeping, or waking up still feeling tired. There are many ways to build positive mental health, including doing things that you are good at and enjoy, developing personal skills to help when dealing with people, investigating new ways to cope with everyday problems, getting involved with clubs, committees, causes, helping others, occasionally taking risks and trying new things, and having fun and enjoying yourself.

"Suffering from stress" means to feel anxiety and tension. Situations that we perceive as difficult, dangerous, or painful can all cause stress. A certain amount of stress does us no harm. However, if people let stress overwhelm them, it can cause physical illness. It is important to understand some ways to decrease stress. These include exercising, doing relaxing things, eating regularly and healthily, breaking difficult tasks into small steps, talking to someone, or thinking positive things about yourself.

1 What makes you feel stressed?

2 What "warning signs" show that you are stressed?

3 How well do you feel you cope with stress?

4 Read the scenarios below with a small group. Discuss the following questions.

- What is causing the person to feel stressed?
- What are the "warning signs" showing each person is stressed?
- Suggest what each person could do to manage the felt stress.

Report your answers to the class.

> Jody always runs out of time to do her homework. During the week, she is busy with basketball, music, and dance classes, and is also expected to look after her baby brother after school two afternoons a week. Jody spends a lot of time talking on the phone to her friends, but she doesn't want to give that up. Jody's teachers have started keeping her in at recess so she can finish her homework. She begins bursting into tears very easily and finds she is short-tempered.

> Shani hates going to parties. She always feels like she wears the wrong clothes and is worried everyone will laugh at her. At the last party she went to, she felt clumsy and couldn't think of anything to say. She ended up hiding in the bathroom for most of the night. She would love to enjoy parties, but doesn't know what to do.

> Mark has an important music exam coming up. The closer the date gets, the worse he feels. He gets stomach cramps every time he thinks about the exam and finds his practice sessions are not going well. He often feels short of breath during his lessons. He really wants to take the exam because he wants to work as a professional musician one day.

> Jeremy finds taking exams very difficult. No matter how well he has prepared, he finds he can't concentrate on what he is writing, his knees feel shaky, and sometimes he has to read questions three or four times before they make any sense. Jeremy's results are usually good, but it doesn't seem to make any difference to the way he copes with exams.

Indicators

- Evaluates current time-management practices.
- Establishes time-management strategies which incorporate aspects of a healthy lifestyle.

The lesson

Discussion points:

- How would you rate how busy your life is on a scale of 1–10, if 10 is "super-busy"?
- How would you rate your ability to manage your time?
- What types of tasks do you do every day? Every week? Every month?
- Do particular people have expectations of you to get certain things done? Explain.
- What is important to you to include in your regular weekly program?
- What types of things do you never seem to get time to do?

What to do:

- Prior to completing this activity, it would be helpful if students could keep an activity log for 3–7 days. From the time they wake up to the time they go to sleep, record all activity: the time each activity was started, finished and the total time it took. At the end of each day, ask students to highlight the activities that were a priority and circle the activities that could have been done at any time.
- Discuss the first two points above.
- Organize the class into small groups to discuss their activity logs. Ask students to make note of the types of activities they have recorded in their log and if any of the activities could be considered time wasters.
- Direct students to complete Question 1 on the worksheet, ordering their most common time-wasting activities from most to least.
- Discuss the remaining points above. Be sure to record student responses on the board as a ready reference for ideas to help them complete the worksheet.
- Students may need to refer to their activity logs to evaluate and complete the worksheet.
- Students should be encouraged to put their plans into practice over the following week. Each student should evaluate how well he/she managed his/her time. Compare the level of achievement of tasks to weeks where a timetable was not used to manage time.

Answers:

Answers will vary

Additional Activities

- Students can set themselves daily to-do lists, weekly plans, term plans and year plans to achieve specified tasks, goals and activities.
- Each student can work with a mentor to achieve his/her goals, receive support and encouragement, and make himself/herself accountable to someone else to ensure goals are met.
- Encourage students to develop time-management skills by setting aside one afternoon each week for using open learning strategies. Set the students some tasks which can be completed in the set time. It is up to them to prioritize the tasks and allocate adequate time to complete them.

Background Information

Effective time-management strategies are learned—they are not innate. It takes practice to get the formula right.

The first step to effective time management is to set goals and to prioritize these according to your set of values. Goals may be long-term, short-term, or immediate.

There is no right way to manage your time; it is learning about yourself, making decisions and following through to achieve your goals.

A process which could be put in place to manage time effectively could be:

- Make a list of tasks to be completed in the coming week.
- Estimate how long each task will take.
- Identify the day you will attend to and complete each task.
- Write a to-do list at the beginning of each day.
- Assess your priorities as you write your daily to-do list.
- Evaluate your to-do list each morning and night.

Things to consider when planning goals:

- Time spent eating and sleeping.
- Time spent traveling to and from school and out-of-school activities.
- Time spent at school and on out-of-school activities.
- Amount of time required to complete household chores.
- Time spent exercising, being with friends and family, watching TV and completing homework.

Did you know there are 168 hours in every week? How well do you use your time?

1 Make a list of the top five ways you waste your time.

(a) _____

(b) _____

(c) _____

(d) _____

(e) _____

2 Write a list of tasks which must done in the coming week; e.g., homework, chores, school, sports. Write them in order of importance. Be sure to include the amount of time you expect each task to take.

Order of importance	Task	Time

3 Plan a timetable which includes these weekly tasks, some things you would like to do, time spent with friends and some exercise.

Time	Sunday	Monday	Tuesday	Wednesday	Thursday	Friday	Saturday
7:00 a.m.							
8:00 a.m.							
9:00 a.m.							
10:00 a.m.							
11:00 a.m.							
noon							
1:00 p.m.							
2:00 p.m.							
3:00 p.m.							
4:00 p.m.							
5:00 p.m.							
6:00 p.m.							
7:00 p.m.							
8:00 p.m.							

Indicators

- Gains an understanding of the term "fair play."
- Values fair play.

The Lesson

Discussion points:

- What is fair play?
- Sometimes it can be difficult to play fairly. Discuss.
- Why are rules important in sports?
- Should you always accept an umpire's decision? Why?
- Can you demonstrate fair play in areas other than sports? Give examples.

What to do:

- Ask the class to brainstorm a list of words and phrases they think of when they hear the term "fair play." Ask why it might be important to a sports team. They could also give examples they have seen of fair play, and examples of when someone has not played fair.
- Read the text at the top of the page and discuss to ensure the students understand the meaning of each point before answering Questions 1 and 2.
- Question 3 can be answered independently.
- Students should work independently to answer Questions 4 and 5. Some volunteers could read aloud what they wrote on their certificates.

Answers:

Teacher check

Additional Activities

- Ask students to watch televised sports matches and write examples of how fair the players were.
- Write sets of "fair play" rules for the classroom, for the home, etc.
- Small groups of students could write and perform their own radio commentary for part of an imaginary sports game. They should remark on the fairness of the players during the commentary.

Background Information

Fairness means treating others the way you want to be treated. Fair-minded people play by the rules and don't take advantage of others. When playing games or sports, it is important that students know that, although competition is fun and motivational, winning shouldn't always be the focus. Through game-playing, students learn skills such as communication, problem solving and self-management.

To play fair, students need to:

1. *Respect the rules.*
2. *Respect the officials and their decisions.*
3. *Give everybody an equal chance to participate.*
4. *Respect their opponent(s).*
5. *Maintain their self-control at all times.*

Imagine you have just joined a sports team. The coach gives you this information.

> ## Fair Play
>
> We expect fair play from all team members.
> This means:
> * Playing by the rules.
> * Accepting the umpire's decisions.
> * Giving everybody an equal chance to participate.
> * Respecting your opponents.
> * Maintaining your self-control at all times.

1 Why do you think you should play by the rules and accept the umpire's decisions?

_____

_____

_____

_____

2 Why do you think everybody should be given an equal chance to participate?

_____

_____

_____

_____

3 Give an example of one way you could:

(a) respect your opponents _____

(b) maintain your self-control _____

4 Rate how important you think fair play is. Write why you chose this rating.

extremely	very	somewhat	not very	not at all
◯	◯	◯	◯	◯

_____

_____

5 Congratulations! You have played your first game with the team and have been given the "Fairest Player" award. Write a certificate which describes some of the things you did during the match to receive the award. The sport you played can be your favorite sport.

> ### Fairest Player Award
>
> Awarded to: _____
>
> For: _____
>
> _____
>
> _____

Indicators

- Participates in teamwork activities requiring cooperation and communication.
- Identifies the qualities of good teamwork.
- Evaluates teamwork performance of his/her group.

The Lesson

Discussion points:

- How did your group cooperate?
- What problems did your group encounter? How were they solved?
- What are good group work qualities?
- What are good leadership qualities?
- Were you happy with your group's performance? Why/Why not?

What to do:

- Divide the class into groups of five or six. Students will be given an activity to complete and evaluate. The groups who work well collaboratively will be more successful.
- Explain to the students that talking to group members is vital to complete the activity successfully. The whole group must agree on each decision before it is carried out.
- Explain the following activity to the students.

  Objects and shapes
  - Each of the following objects or shapes is to be made in their group.
  - Every group member should be part of the object or shape.
  - Each person must hold his/her pose for at least ten seconds.

  Choose from the following (or use your own). You must use at least four.
  - a pentagon or hexagon
  - an irregular shape (hold up a diagram or draw on the board)
  - a camel   – a monster   – a couch   – an elephant
  - a can opener   – a cloths pin   – egg beaters   – a car
  - a bicycle   – a television

- Students should complete the activity without viewing the other teams.
- When the activity is completed, each group can present a selection of the shapes or objects to the class.
- Read through Question 1 with the whole class. Discuss the list of considerations before students complete the question individually. Responses can be shared and discussed within their groups.
- Question 2 can be completed within these groups. Common keywords and phrases can be listed on the board.
- Questions 3 to 4 should be completed individually after being read through and the meaning of unfamiliar words discussed. Leadership qualities can be listed as above.

Answers:

Teacher check

Additional Activities

- Repeat the activity using a different group combination.
- Write dictionary definitions for words used in Questions 2 and 3.
- List teams/groups in which each student is involved.

Background Information

The qualities of an effective team include:

Working towards a clear goal—*the team clearly understands and works towards the goal that is to be achieved. Team members are focused on the tasks they are assigned by the team. The team defines any targets that need to be achieved as it works towards the common goal.*

Good communication—*the team members listen to each other with respect and willingly share their ideas without domination. Through this, the team members develop a mutual trust. Logical decisions are made with the acceptance of all team members.*

Consideration—*the team members encourage and support each other's ideas, giving critical feedback. Any criticism is aimed at the idea, rather than the person who contributed the idea. This encourages a willingness for the team to take risks and create new ideas. Everyone has an important role in the team.*

The activities on the worksheet foster team skills such as communication, cooperation, negotiation, working towards a goal, problem-solving, allocating tasks, performing leadership roles, risk taking and creative thinking. They will also reinforce the concept that team members depend on each other for the whole team to work well.

1 Now you have completed the shapes and objects activity, finish the evaluation below to see how well you and your team did.

Consider the following questions when commenting.

- Did the team have a clear understanding of the task?
- Did everyone participate?
- How was this done?
- Did someone become a leader? If so, how did they perform this role?

- Were problems discussed and dealt with?
- Did team members listen to each other?
- Did everyone agree with the decisions?

Team Evaluation

Team members: Task:

_____   _____

_____   _____

_____   _____

Comment on and rate how well the task was completed by your team (10 being the best).

1	2	3	4	5	6	7	8	9	10

_____

_____

You will have noticed that each team did not work in quite the same way.
Some of the teams would have worked cooperatively, some would have worked in a disorganized way, and some may have had a team member take on the role of a leader.

2 From what you have learned from this activity, list keywords and phrases to describe the qualities of a good team.

3 Circle the qualities below you think would describe a good leader. Add more of your own.

disorganized	*kind*	*bossy*
a good listener	*in control*	*helpful*
gives suggestions	*organized*	*polite*
includes everyone	*confident*	*rude*
well-spoken	*focused*	*loud*
assertive	*passive*	*timid*
understanding		

4 How do you think you perform as a member of a team?

_____

_____

5 How do you think you perform as a team leader?

_____

_____

Indicators

- Understands what is meant by "effective communication."
- Considers how well he/she communicates with others.

The Lesson

Discussion points:

- What skills does a good communicator have?
- How important are listening skills?
- With whom do you find it easiest to communicate?
- With whom do you find it most difficult to communicate?
- Do you think people find it easier to communicate with others as they get older? Explain.
- Which factors prevent successful communication?
- Which factors promote successful communication?

What to do:

- Students will need to work with a partner for Question 2. Before the activity begins, each pair will need to decide who will play "A" and who will play "B." The scenarios below can then be cut out and distributed. Instruct the students to look only at their own sheet of paper.

> You (A) are working on a school project where you have to design a public information poster on road safety with your partner (B). You feel the poster should be suitable for all ages to see. You want the poster to be colorful and appealing with a catchy, rhyming slogan. You also want to include some humor. You feel that if people are entertained and made to feel happy, they will take more notice of the information.

> You (B) are working on a school project where you have to design a public information poster on road safety with your partner (A). You feel the poster should be suitable only for adults. You want the poster to be hard-hitting, with gloomy colors and frightening images. You also want to include some grim statistics. You feel that if people are shocked, they will take more notice of the information.

Answers:

Answers will vary

Additional Activities

- Hold a lesson in which only nonverbal communication can be used. How easy is it to get messages across?
- Play drama games in which students have to use good listening skills.

Background Information

Appropriate communication skills are vital to developing interpersonal relationships. Verbal and nonverbal methods of communication include: facial expressions, body language, and tone, volume and clarity of voice.

Listening is a skill vital in all areas of learning. It may be learned and developed in a number of ways. Listening to audio tapes and stories, following directions, listening to instructions, and repeating messages are some activities which help to develop communication skills.

Communication is a two-way process.
When we communicate with someone, we both send and receive messages.
This can be done verbally or nonverbally (e.g., using gestures or body language).

Look at the diagram.

sending message

communicating thoughts, ideas or feelings; e.g., making a speech, stamping foot, smiling, etc.

receiving message

actively listening to message sender and giving feedback; e.g., nodding, frowning, arguing, etc.

1 List the qualities you think an effective communicator has.
Consider both sending and receiving messages.

2 To "actively listen" to someone is not the same as just hearing what he/she says. Find a partner to work with. Read the scenario you are given. Don't look at your partner's!
Imagine your two characters meet.

- Take turns to tell each other your opinions and feelings about the poster design.

- Restate your partner's ideas to show you have listened and suggest a compromise.

3 Rate how well you feel your partner listened to you.

O————O————O————O————O————O————O
poor   average   excellent

4 How highly do you value the skill of listening? Give a reason for your answer.

5 (a) Sometimes we can find it difficult to communicate with some people.
Name three barriers to successful communication.

(b) Suggest ways these barriers could be overcome.

6 Name three people you feel you can effectively communicate with and write some topics you usually communicate about; e.g., problems at school, your favorite music, family problems, etc.

Name of person	Topics

7 How well do you think you communicate? Give reasons. (Discuss with a partner.)

Indicators

- Understands the importance of family.
- Considers the relationships within his/her own family.

The Lesson

Discussion points:

- Why are families so important?
- Who is in your family?
- Who are you closest to in your family? Why?
- How would you describe your family?
- How can families help us?
- What kinds of things do you do for your family?
- How does your family deal with family disagreements?
- What special things do you do with your family?

What to do:

- Discuss the questions above before reading the text at the top of the page.
- Read Question 1 together as a class. Ask students to give examples of physical and "other" things done for them by their families. "Other" things should include emotional support, such as being comforted when upset, celebrating achievements, etc.
- If students require more room when answering Question 3, direct them to use the back of the page.
- After students have completed Questions 1 to 6, you may like to discuss Question 5 and ask students to describe how their family would deal with the disagreements. This will help students to understand that all families are different. Students could role-play how different families deal with the disagreements.
- A word chart could be made from the answers to Question 6 and displayed in the classroom.

Answers:

Answers will vary

Additional Activities

- Students write a poem to show how they feel about their family.
- Students write about their families' interests; e.g., music, tennis, hiking, camping, etc.
- Students write words or phrases that describe the best things about their family.

Background Information

Our family is the first group of people with whom we form a relationship. A lot of how we think and feel about different things comes from what we learn within our families. We often change our behavior depending on who we are relating to. The way we speak to friends, colleagues, parents, grandparents and strangers varies. The way we act is influenced by what is expected of us. Authority figures, such as teachers, police officers, etc., expect us to obey and respect them and, normally, we do. Some children may have a similar relationship with their parents. Others may not feel they are expected to obey and respect their parents for a number of reasons. For many families, a lack of communication can be the reason for misunderstood expectations.

The first and most important relationships you have are with members of your family.
They can provide you with the opportunities to discover new things and develop as a person.

1 Make a list of things your family does for you. You should include physical things (e.g., providing food) and any other things you can think of. Rank the items on your list in order of importance to you (1 is the most important).

Things my family does for me	Rank
physical	
other	

2 Give three examples of important things you do for different members of your family.

Name	Relationship	Important thing

3 Sometimes families try to help us by commenting on our actions. Write some helpful comments your family has made about you recently. They can be positive or negative.

4 How do you usually react when negative comments are made about you by your family?

5 Write how your family might deal with each of these family disagreements.

- where to take a family vacation

- how much allowance is given

Indicators

- Reviews current and past friendships.
- Evaluates himself/herself as a person in order to develop friendships.
- Establishes strategies to make new friendships while maintaining existing friendships.

The Lesson

Discussion points:

- What type of friend are you? (Consider the skills in the Background Information when discussing this question.)
- What qualities do you look for in a friend? Explain why.
- How can you make new friends?
- Why would you want to make new friends?
- Do you ever feel left out? Explain the situations or reasons for these feelings.
- How do friendships change with members of the opposite sex as you grow older?
- How do you cope with changes in your friendships?

Materials needed/Preparation:

- Letter-sized sheets of butcher paper
- Organize students into groups of five or six

What to do:

- Begin by discussing the first question from the Discussion points. Offer students information about the skills involved in being a good friend from the Background Information. Encourage students to describe themselves as a friend.
- Distribute sheets of butcher paper and ask students to record keywords and phrases to describe their current friendships on one side. Are they happy and positive? Do they feel they are an equal or are they the leader? On the other side record the same information about past friendships. Have the students discuss the information recorded on the sheet with their peers, in small groups.
- Direct students to Question 1 on the worksheet. This activity may require some real soul-searching for some students, while others may find it easy. Read through the adjectives and explain any terms students may not understand before asking them to complete the activity.
- Discuss the second question from the Discussion points in small groups. Students then complete Question 2 on the worksheet. Encourage students to share some of their words and record these on the board. Discuss whether there were some common qualities all students looked for in a friend.
- Discuss the third and fourth questions from the Discussion points as a whole class. Students then complete Questions 3 and 4 on the worksheet.

Answers:

Answers will vary

Additional Activities

- Students can work in pairs to role-play how they would begin to develop a new friendship.
- Write a newspaper advertisement looking for a new friend. Students will need to clearly and succinctly describe the qualities they are looking for in a friend.
- Discuss the fifth and sixth questions from the Discussion points in small groups and report main ideas to the whole class.
- Students discuss and draw a map to show how friendships change over time and include brief explanations of their mechanisms for coping with the changes.

Background Information

Friendships can be extraordinary if carefully nurtured. Good, solid friendships are an important component in a feeling of self-worth and belonging.

Choosing people to be friends with often demonstrates a person's own understanding of himself/herself. For example, people who have a positive self-image tend to attract people who also have a positive self-image; people who have low self-esteem tend to attract people who also have low self-esteem. It is important that individuals take time to get to know themselves before they can know what to look for in a friend.

In order to evaluate friendships, it is important to develop the skills involved in maintaining positive friendships. These can be listed as:

- *Talk with and listen to friends, be interested.*
- *Give positive feedback.*
- *Always use manners and be kind and considerate.*
- *Be dependable, respectful, honest and trustworthy.*
- *Help each other solve problems.*
- *Understand each other's feelings and moods.*
- *Allow for differences in opinion, giving each other the opportunity to express thoughts, feelings and ideas.*
- *Give each other room to change and grow.*

1 You need to evaluate yourself as a person before you can determine the types of people you would like to choose as friends.
Circle as many words as you need to in each category that you think best describe you. You can also add your own words, if necessary.

My nature

loving	sharing	friendly
giving	considerate	outspoken
generous	patient	argumentative
hard-working	loyal	thoughtful
caring	well-mannered	funny
shy	polite	interested in others
happy	gentle	
quiet	approachable	
outgoing	honest	
trustworthy	interesting	
helpful	cooperative	

My interests/hobbies

watching TV	walking	animals
computers	sewing	acting
crafts	games	outdoor activities
playing games	reading	
school	writing	
music	swimming	
team sports	camping	
dancing	bike riding	
cooking	art	
making models	nature	

2 Think about the qualities you would look for in a friend. You may use some of the words from above or write your own. List as many as you can in the space below.

When you meet someone for the first time, it can be a bit awkward. Both people are unsure how to behave or talk, or even unsure whether you have anything in common with each other. Things need to move slowly—best friends are not made overnight!

3 So now you know what qualities you would look for in a friend. Let's say you have met a person you think has some of these qualities. How would you begin to develop a friendship?

_____

_____

_____

4 Below are some steps which could be used when developing a new friendship. Check the ones you would use.

☐ *Ask him/her about himself/herself.*

☐ *Be a good listener to show that you are interested.*

☐ *Be a positive person.*

☐ *Be cruel and gossip about your new friend.*

☐ *Share "safe" thoughts and interests first.*

☐ *Be highly opinionated and argue with everything he/she says.*

☐ *Be thoughtful and helpful.*

☐ *Be bossy and boastful when talking with your friend.*

☐ *Spend time with him/her and get to know him/her as a person.*

☐ *Expect him/her to spend all his/her time with you.*

Indicators

- Reviews current and past friendships.
- Evaluates what characteristics are important to him/her.
- Establishes strategies to make new friendships and maintain existing friendships.

The Lesson

Discussion points:

- What type of friend are you? (Consider the skills in the Background Information when discussing this question.)
- What qualities do you look for in a friend? Explain why.
- How can you make new friends?
- Why would you want to make new friends?
- Are all your friendships the same? Explain.

What to do:

- Have each student brainstorm and record as many words and phrases as possible to describe himself/herself; e.g., loving, giving, generous, caring, happy, quiet, outgoing, shy, considerate, etc. Discuss the words he/she listed with his/her peers and see if the other students can add to the list.
- Discuss the first point above. Offer students information about the skills involved in being a good friend from the Background Information. Encourage students to describe themselves as a friend.
- Students then complete Question 1 on the worksheet. Use only keywords and phrases, as space is limited. If students have difficulty, allow them to seek the advice of a friend in the class for a brief discussion.
- Discuss the second point above and then ask students to complete Question 2 on the worksheet. Remind students that it is their own personal choice and there are no right or wrong answers.
- Discuss points three and four above. Talk about how some people have difficulties making new friends. Think about why these people have trouble and how they must feel.
- Students can then offer suggestions by completing Question 3. This activity makes the students aware of strategies to use to make new friends and how they could be more open to students who are not as skilled in this area as themselves.
- Students then complete Question 4 independently. Organize the students into small groups to discuss the various strategies recorded.
- Discuss the final point. Students may discover through this discussion that they have different friends for different purposes; e.g., one student may have a friend from weekend sports, so when they get together, they generally talk about sports, etc. Another friend may be from school, so they generally talk about things going on at school, activities, projects, etc.; another friend might be the ideal person to share secrets with. On closer inspection, students may be surprised how they share different aspects of their lives with different people and how differently they act with particular people.

Answers:

Answers will vary

Additional Activities

- Work in pairs to role-play how they would establish a new friendship.
- Write a note to your friend telling him/her why you think he/she is such great friend.

Background Information

Friendships can be extraordinary if carefully nurtured. Good, solid friendships are an important component of a feeling of self-worth and belonging.

Choosing people to be friends with often demonstrates a person's own understanding of himself/herself; i.e. people who have a positive self-image tend to attract people who also have a positive self-image; people who have low self-esteem tend to attract people who also have low self-esteem. It is important that individuals take the time to get to know themselves before they can expect to know what to look for in a friend.

To be able to evaluate friendships, it is important to know the skills involved in maintaining positive friendships. These can be listed as:

- *Talk with friends about common interests, current issues, etc.*
- *Share conversations so each person gets the chance to talk and the chance to listen.*
- *Listen, be interested in what he/she has to say and ask questions.*
- *Give friends positive feedback when they do something well, avoid put-downs.*
- *Always use manners and be kind and considerate.*
- *Be dependable, respectful, honest and trustworthy.*
- *Help each other solve problems.*
- *Understand feelings and moods.*
- *Allow for differences in opinion; give the opportunity to express himself/herself without hurting the other person.*
- *Give each other room to change and grow.*

1 Review your current and past friendships.
Consider the type of friend you are, the types of friends you spend time with and your ability to maintain steady friendships.

Current friendships	Past friendships

2 Rank the following to show what is important to you when you choose a friend.

☐ *honesty*	☐ *patience*	☐ *dependability*	☐ *good communication skills*
☐ *sports ability*	☐ *loyalty*	☐ *leadership*	☐ *common interests*
☐ *money*	☐ *trust*	☐ *popularity*	☐ *appearance*

Some people have difficulty making new friends.
They may be shy, lack confidence, or have moved often.

3 What advice would you give to someone who has a hard time making new friends?

_____

_____

_____

_____

4 Describe the best ways of keeping friends and making new friends.

Indicators

- Explores different types of relationships: child/parent, child/teacher, child/child.
- Identifies different standards of behavior in different relationships.
- Identifies the expectations placed on him/her in different relationships.

The Lesson

Discussion points:

- What is a relationship?
- With whom do you have relationships?
- What do you value about your relationships?
- Do you always act the same way in all of your relationships?
- Do different people have different expectations of you?
- What are your expectations of different people?

Materials needed/Preparation:

- Letter-sized sheets of butcher paper
- Organize students into groups of five or six

What to do:

- Begin by discussing the first question from the Discussion points in groups. Students then report their ideas to the class. Students can then record their definition of a relationship in Question 1.
- Discuss the second question from the Discussion points. Provide students with butcher paper. Ask them to draw a circle in the center and write "me" inside it. They then draw branches out from this circle and record all the people with whom they have a relationship.
- Discuss the idea that we have different relationships with different people, and there may be certain things we particularly value about each relationship. Pose the question "What do you value about your relationships?" Students add this information underneath each person's name on their chart.
- Read Question 2 on the worksheet. With a partner, students can discuss how they act in different relationships. For example, students will act differently at home from when they are at school. Discuss as a class the types of words we can use to describe our behavior and record these on the board for the students to refer to when completing the activity. Students can then complete the table using relevant keywords and phrases.
- Discuss the final two Discussion points as a whole class and emphasize that expectations go both ways. For example, teachers expect students to make eye contact when talking, to follow the classroom rules, to be organized, to complete tasks to their best ability, to finish work on time, and to use good manners. Students also have expectations of their teachers; for example, to be treated with respect, to learn new things, to be organized, and to be helpful when they have a problem.
- Students can then complete Questions 3 and 4 on the worksheet.

Answers:

Answers will vary

Additional Activities

- Students can discuss in small groups any particular problems they may have in a relationship and work together to devise possible solutions.
- Role-play in small groups scenarios of behavior in different situations involving different relationships.
- Write a letter to a person you have a relationship with and let them know what you admire about them and what you value about your relationship.
- If you had the opportunity to change any aspect of one of your relationships, what would it be? How would you change it? Why would you want to change it?

Background Information

Every day we spend time with many different people. Each person "expects" us to behave in a different way. Our parents have expectations and so do friends, teachers, coaches and acquaintances. We are able to adjust our behavior slightly depending on the relationship we have with a person. The way we speak with our friends is quite different from how we would speak to our teachers.

Communication is the key to developing good, strong relationships with many different people. It is important to be able to discuss issues, solve conflicts, negotiate and make decisions. We need to know how to express our thoughts and feelings but not to force them on others.

Good relationships with anyone rely on having a good level of respect for each other, being able to communicate clearly, and on building a high level of trust over time.

1 What is a relationship?

2 List keywords and phrases to describe your behavior when you are in the company of …

Me

a teacher/coach	a parent	close friend	someone you have just met

3 Write the expectations placed on you by your …

(a) *teacher.* _____

_____

_____

(b) *parent(s).* _____

_____

_____

(c) *peers.* _____

_____

_____

(d) *closest friend.* _____

_____

4 Write the expectations you place on your …

(a) *teacher.* _____

_____

_____

(b) *parent(s).* _____

_____

_____

(c) *peers.* _____

_____

_____

(d) *closest friend.* _____

_____

Indicators

- Explores different types of relationships: child/parent, child/teacher, child/child.
- Identifies different standards of behavior in different relationships.
- Identifies the expectations placed on him/her in different relationships.

The Lesson

Discussion points:

- What is a relationship?
- With whom do you have a relationship?
- Do you always act the same way in all of your relationships?
- Do different people have different expectations of you?
- What are your expectations of different people?
- What do you value about your relationships?

What to do:

- Discuss the first point above and work together to develop a sentence to define the term "relationship." Record this sentence on the board.
- Direct students to complete the brainstorming activity in Question 1 on the worksheet. Then discuss the second discussion point.
- Review the types of qualities the students looked for in a friend. Some of these may be used to complete Question 2. Ask students to rank the qualities they list in order of most important to least important.
- Discuss points three, four and five above. Encourage open discussion and the provision of examples. Different expectations within a relationship affect the way we act in that relationship. Expectations go both ways in a relationship. For example, parents have certain expectations of their children and children have certain expectations of their parents.
- Students can then complete the remainder of the worksheet. Some relationships are more pleasurable than others; students need to evaluate this and define why some relationships are preferred over others.
- Conclude the lesson with a discussion about the final point. Students could work in small groups to develop a poster which displays keywords and key phrases about what they value in their relationships. This will provide a handy reference for students when trying to establish or maintain positive relationships with the people around them.

Answers:

Answers will vary

Additional Activities

- Role-play in small groups scenarios of behavior in different situations involving different relationships.
- Write a note to someone who you have a relationship with and tell him/her why you enjoy your relationship.
- Write a poem about a relationship you have or have had in the past.
- Develop a "steps to follow" plan to building and maintaining a positive relationship with another person.

Background Information

Every day we spend time with many different people. Each person "expects" us to behave in a different way. Our parents have expectations, and so do friends, teachers, coaches, acquaintances, etc. We are able to adjust our behavior slightly depending on the relationship we have with each person. The way we speak with our friends is quite different from how we speak to our teachers.

Communication is the key to developing good, strong relationships with many different people. It is important to be able to discuss issues, raise conflicts, negotiate, and make decisions. We need to know how to express our thoughts and feelings but not to force them on others.

Good relationships with anyone rely on a significant level of respect for each other, being able to communicate clearly, and building a high level of trust over time.

1 On the diagram, write all the relationships you have with people; e.g., teacher, parent, friend, etc.

2 What do you think are the qualities people need to ensure they develop positive relationships?

_____

_____

_____

_____

_____

Yes	No

3 Think about your relationships. Do you act the same way in each of them? List three relationships and explain how you behave and speak in each one.

Relationship	How I behave and speak

(Do not name the person, just the relationship; e.g., mother, father, friend, cousin, teacher, etc.)

4 Describe your favorite relationship. (Do not name the person, just the relationship; e.g., mother, father, friend, cousin, teacher, etc.)

_____

_____

5 Make a list of why this relationship is your favorite.

6 Describe your least favorite relationship. (Do not name the person, just the relationship; e.g., mother, father, friend, cousin, teacher, etc.)

_____

7 Why this relationship is your least favorite?

_____

8 How could you improve this relationship?

_____

Indicators

- Completes questions about empathy.
- Interviews another student to gain some understanding of his/her feelings, attitudes, likes and dislikes.

The Lesson

Discussion points:

- How well do you know the other students in the class?
- Do you think that if you knew more about them, you may understand why they say, feel, or do the things they do?
- How do you feel when you hear a sad or tragic news story? Do you think about how the people involved may be feeling?
- Is "sympathy" the same as "empathy"? Use your dictionary to find the answer.

What to do:

- Read the poem or ask an individual student to read it to the class. Discuss the poem, ensuring that students fully understand what it is about. Students complete Questions 2 to 4. A dictionary is needed to answer Question 2.
- Students form pairs to complete Questions 5 and 6. It is best to form pairs from students who don't know each other well. Students may share their answers to Questions 1 to 4 with the class and discuss answers. Interview sheets may be shown to the teacher if given permission by the student who was interviewed.

Answers:

Answers will vary

Additional Activities

- Read scenarios about how students may feel in different situations. Would you feel the same?
- Recall some sad news stories such as the tsunami of 2004. Did you feel sorry for families who lost brothers, sisters, mothers, fathers, sons and daughters? Can you imagine how it would feel if someone in your family had been hurt or killed there?
- Allow students to relate good things that have happened to them. Sometimes good news must be shared immediately.
- Allow talking and listening times within the class, with a one- or two-minute time limit, for students to share news with others.
- Choose a student of the week. Students prepare and display a biography about themselves.

Background Information

Empathy means "mentally entering into the feeling or spirit of a person or thing." Simply speaking, "empathy" means to feel sympathetic towards another person or to be in accord with him/her. For children this means putting themselves in someone else's place and imagining how that person feels. Students need to be appreciative and tolerant of differences in others. It is sometimes easier to ridicule the unknown or unfamiliar than to show sympathy and understanding.

1 (a) Read the poem below.

> *If I had to walk in your shoes*
> *My socks would slip and my heels would bruise.*
> *Your shoes are too big and mine are too small*
> *Can we really understand each other at all?*
> *Wouldn't it be great; wouldn't it be cool*
> *To follow this golden rule!*
> *"If you want to know how another person feels*
> *Put yourself in their place" (but mind the heels!)*

(b) What is the poem about?

_____

_____

_____

_____

2 Look up the word "empathy" in a dictionary and write the meaning.

_____

_____

_____

3 Why is it important to be able to put yourself in someone else's place?

_____

_____

_____

4 Give an example of a time when you really wanted to know how another person was feeling.

_____

_____

_____

Learning about another person helps us to understand how they are feeling and why they do things. We learn to accept and appreciate their similarities and differences.

5 Choose a student in your class who you don't know very well. Interview the student and complete the questions below.

(a) What are the things you like the most?

(b) What are the things you dislike the most?

(c) What is the worst thing that has happened to you?

(d) What is the best thing that has happened to you?

6 Read your report to the student who was interviewed to see whether you recorded the information correctly. Do not share this information with anyone else unless you are given permission from the student who was interviewed.

Indicators

- Gains an understanding of the types of expectations and assumptions people can have about boys and girls.
- Considers what effects these expectations and assumptions can have on people's lives.

The Lesson

Discussion points:

- What is a stereotype? Can you think of any stereotypes of people? Examples might include, ALL people who do well at school are boring, ALL people who live in big expensive houses are snobs, etc.
- What kinds of stereotypical ideas do some people have about boys and girls or men and women? Are any or all of them fair? How do they make you feel?
- Discuss why it is important that we are all treated as individuals.
- Have you ever been in a situation where you have been stereotyped? Explain.

What to do:

- Explain the term "gender" and what is meant by expectations and assumptions. Students could give some examples by completing these statements "Girls are often expected to…," "It is usually assumed that boys are…."
- Read the text at the top of the page and the diary entry. You may like several students to share reading the diary entry aloud to the class. Discuss the ideas in the diary entry before students complete Question 1.
- Ask volunteers to read out their answers to Question 1. Before asking students to form small groups, discuss how the ideas given might affect people. You may need to give some examples; e.g., "Girls should learn to cook"–it might stop a girl from practicing something she enjoys or may make her feel angry or annoyed. You could also ask students how such statements make them feel.
- Ask a representative from each group to read out the group's ideas. Write any ideas the groups had in common on the board and discuss.
- Students complete Question 2 and share their answers.

Answers:

1. Students' answers should include at least four of the following (note: the answers may vary slightly):

   - Girls aren't as good at math as boys.
   - Boys are stronger than girls.
   - Boys like to play with remote control cars.
   - Girls are good at sewing.
   - Girls should learn to cook.
   - Girls like clothes.

2. Teacher check

Additional Activities

- Prepare student debates on topics like "Boys shouldn't wear pink," "Girls are gentler than boys," etc.
- Ask students to conduct a survey consisting of a number of stereotypical statements about boys and girls. They should instruct groups of students from different grades to check "disagree," "unsure," or "agree" for each statement, as in Question 1 on the activity page. Compile the results and discuss. Graphs or charts can be made showing how children of different ages responded to the statements.

Background Information

This activity focuses on expectations and assumptions people can have about boys and girls. You may like to introduce the term "stereotype" when students are completing the activity. A stereotype can be described as a very simple—and often incorrect—picture that people have of a particular person. Stereotypes depend on conventional ideas about groups of people which may include attitudes, interests, characteristic traits, or physical features.

As some expectations of and assumptions about of boys and girls are cultural, you will need to exercise sensitivity when approaching this activity. A discussion about customs and beliefs prevalent in different cultures could be useful and would also tie in with the theme of stereotypes.

©World Teachers Press®

Are Boys and Girls Always Treated the Same?

Sometimes boys and girls are treated differently simply because of their gender. This can affect people's opinions of themselves and what they feel they can achieve or should do.

Read this diary entry.

Dear Diary,

Today is my birthday (and Jackson's too, being my twin) but I can't say it has been a happy day so far. In math, I answered a question incorrectly, and Sam teased me that girls aren't as good as boys at math. This made me steaming mad!

During our art lesson, we did some sewing. The teacher held up James' sewing as the best in the class. He looked so embarrassed! I heard a group of boys tease him that sewing was something only girls are good at. When I talked to James after school, he said he will sew badly next week so he doesn't get teased again.

After school, Jackson and I helped Mom get ready for our party. I had to help with the food (same as every year) while Jackson moved the furniture outside. I'm just as strong as he is! Why can't Mom see that? She thinks girls should have to learn to cook. I hate it!

Finally, we were allowed to open our presents. Most of them were great. The only one I didn't like was Aunty Dee's. I can't believe she sent me clothes! She gave Jackson a cool remote control car. I'm so jealous. Maybe he'll let me have a turn later.

Now it's time for the party to begin. I hope it makes up for the rest of the day!

Imogen

1 Write at least four of the ideas the people in Imogen's diary have about boys or girls; e.g., "Girls like clothes." Check a box to show how you feel about each one.

Idea	Agree	Unsure	Disagree

2 In groups, consider how ideas like these might affect someone's feelings or actions. Write your ideas in note form on the back of this page.

Indicators

- Understands the meaning of the term "stereotype."
- Identifies and describes stereotypes in real life and on television.
- Realizes the way people are treated according to a stereotype can affect their self-concept.

The Lesson

Discussion points:

- When you meet someone for the first time, what is the first thing you notice about him/her? Is this the same for people in all age groups you meet?
- What makes you decide you like some people more than others?
- List qualities of your best friends.
- Do you know what someone is really like by appearance alone?
- What is a stereotype?
- Do you wish to be like certain stereotypes? If so, which ones?
- What kind of a person are you?

Materials needed/Preparation:

- Pictures of stereotypical male and female models from magazines and catalogs.

What to do:

- Distribute several of the pictures of stereotypical models to groups of students. Direct them to discuss in their groups what kind of people the pictures represent and why they came to that conclusion.
- Discuss findings as a class. All or most groups should have decided the pictures were of models. List the reasons they came to that conclusion. Discuss other suggested answers, if any.
- Students can complete Question 1 individually.
- Read and discuss the information about a stereotype. Complete Question 2 individually or with a partner. Compare answers within the group. Were they mostly the same or different? Sex of character? Age of character?
- Discuss stereotypes on television. List suggestions given by the students. They can work in pairs to complete Question 3. Ensure they use a range of different programs. Discuss how these stereotypes are treated.
- Relate the treatment of stereotypes to those in real life. Discuss how this can affect someone's self-concept.
- Read through the information relating to Question 4 with the students.
- Students complete the activity and compare answers.

Answers:

Teacher check

Additional Activities

- Students can group themselves according to various categories such as gender; eye, skin, or hair color; birth date or month; food, sports, or hobbies; likes and dislikes; height or weight (be sensitive about this one); and street name or number. This activity will help them realize how we can all fit into different "stereotypes" or categories.
- Write a diary entry of a time you have been part of a stereotypical reaction—to yourself or someone else.

Background Information

A stereotype can be described as a very simple—and often incorrect—picture that people have of a particular type of person. Stereotypes depend on conventional ideas about groups of people which may include attitudes, interests, characteristics, traits, mannerisms, or physical appearance. It is common to base initial judgments about people on stereotypes.

Stereotyping can affect a person's self-concept, when others make unfair assumptions about his/her skills, abilities and behavior. Students need to learn to accept themselves so they can develop an open-minded attitude to others.

Many people compare themselves to others and try to fit into a stereotype. The media has a big influence on creating stereotypes. Television, in particular, uses symbols such as clothing, gestures, settings, physical appearance, behavior and body language to create stereotypes that an audience can easily identify.

1 (a) What did your group decide about the type of person the pictures represented? _____

(b) Explain how your group came to that conclusion. _____

_____

(c) Did all or most groups come to the same conclusion? | yes ___ | no |

Each group based its decision upon recognizing a stereotype.
A stereotype is a fixed idea people have of a particular type of person.
The picture is easily recognized and understood by others who share the same view.

2 (a) Write descriptive words and phrases about what you think each of these people would look like.

A superhero	A rock star	A movie star

(b) Compare your answers with others in your group.

Many stereotypes can be found on television in commercials, soap operas, movies and comedy shows.
Even news programs select certain types of people to be newscasters.

3 Complete the table below, using stereotypical characters from different television programs or commercials.

Character's name and description	TV program/commercial

You have seen the way in which stereotypes are treated on television. For example, popular characters in soap operas have lots of friends. Unpopular characters do not. In real life, people can be treated fairly or unfairly according to the stereotype they appear to be.

4 Read these scenarios and describe how each person might be feeling.

Bree is a very thin girl and quite short for her age. At lunchtimes, a popular game is for girls in her grade to choose teams to play basketball. Bree is nearly always chosen last. Even then, she hardly gets to play and spends most of her time on the bench.	Ramil is new to his school. Being from an Indian background, he has dark hair and skin and brings different foods from home for lunch compared to the other students. He is finding it hard to make friends.

Indicators

- Understands the meaning of the word "stereotype."
- Considers stereotypes in his/her community.
- Considers the meaning of the word "empathy."

The Lesson

Discussion points:

- What is a "stereotype"?
- What can stereotyping lead to?
- Are stereotypes ever fair or useful? Why/Why not?
- Why is it important to be empathetic?
- Is empathy the same as sympathy? Explain.
- Discuss why it is important that we are all treated as individuals.
- Have you ever been in a situation where you have been stereotyped? Explain.

What to do:

- You will need to organize students into groups of four or five before they begin work. Each group will need access to a comprehensive dictionary.
- Depending on the ability of the class, some discussion about stereotypes may be needed before the groups begin work.
- Each group should nominate a spokesperson to give the answers to each of the questions. This should promote class discussion. Teachers should be prepared for words like "racism" and "sexism" to come up.

Answers:

Answers will vary

Additional Activities

- Students could prepare and perform role-plays with stereotypical characters, then perform the same role-play using non-stereotypical characters. They should then consider how the role-play changed.
- Ask the students to watch television programs, particularly soap operas and dramas, and pick out the stereotypical characters. They could discuss whether they think it matters that stereotypical characters are used on television.

Background Information

A stereotype can be described as a very simple—and often incorrect—picture that people have of a particular type of person. Stereotypes depend on conventional ideas about groups of people which may include attitudes, interests, characteristics, traits, mannerisms, or physical appearance. It is common to base initial judgments about people on stereotypes.

Stereotyping can affect a person's self-concept when others make unfair assumptions about his/her skills, abilities and behavior. Students need to learn to accept themselves so they can develop an open-minded attitude toward others.

Many people compare themselves to others and try to fit into the stereotype. The media has a big influence on creating stereotypes. Television, in particular, uses symbols such as clothing, gestures, settings, physical appearance, behavior and body language to create stereotypes that an audience can easily identify.

Stereotyping

A stereotype can be described as a very simple—and often incorrect—picture that people have of a particular type of person. In our communities, people are often stereotyped according to their jobs, gender, disabilities, age, religion, race, culture, or where they live.

In a small group, consider the following.

1 List words to describe a typical stereotype for a person who holds each of these jobs.

(a) airline pilot _____

(b) nurse _____

(c) firefighter _____

(d) garbage collector _____

(e) kindergarten teacher _____

2 Write some further examples of stereotypes you might encounter in your school or community. Try to include some different types; e.g., stereotypes involving older people or the area in which someone lives.

person	stereotype

3 What is the problem with stereotypes? _____

_____

_____

Stereotypes come about through a lack of understanding of those who are different from us.
This can cause people to be teased or ignored.
Showing empathy for people who are different from us is a skill we should all learn.

4 Write what you think the word "empathy" means. You can use a dictionary to help you but write your group's definition in your own words.

_____

5 How can we show empathy for others? Give three examples.

(i) _____

(ii) _____

(iii) _____

Indicator

- Considers the positive and negative effects peer pressure has on influencing behavior and self-concept.

The Lesson

Discussion points:

- What is meant by "peer pressure" and "peer influences"?
- Can peer influences be positive and negative? How?
- List personal positive and negative peer influence experiences.
- How can you say no to a situation you know is wrong?
- How does peer influence affect self-esteem?

What to do:

- Discuss the introductory paragraph with the students.
- Students can work in pairs to answer Questions 1 and 2 before sharing findings with the class. (Some students may not wish to share their answers to Question 2.)
- Discuss Questions 3 to 5 with the class and list keywords and phrases on the board for them to refer to. Students can then answer those questions individually.

Answers:

Teacher check

Additional Activities

- Role-play solutions to the negative scenarios on the activity page. Students can work in groups to prepare the role-plays to perform for the class.
- Discuss how a peer group can influence the following: your appearance, the music you listen to, what you buy with your money, and your entertainment and leisure time.

Background Information

Peer pressure is allowing others to influence your thoughts and actions. People who wish to "belong" to a group are often swayed by peer pressure to follow the group's ideas and actions. Some experts believe that people who feel they belong to a group often feel more confident and their idea of self-worth increases. When in a group, people do not need to make decisions as the group tells them what to do and think.

It is important that people believe in their own self-worth and have confidence in their own thoughts, feelings and actions. People with confidence and who believe in themselves are less likely to be swayed by negative peer pressure.

Peer pressure is not always a bad thing. People can influence others to improve their behavior, such as quitting a bad habit or improving their skills. Some schools have used positive peer pressure to reduce the occurrence of bullying.

> We are all influenced by our peers (people our own age) to some degree.
> This is called "peer pressure."
> Our peers can influence both our thoughts and actions. We do something because "the group" did it instead of making the choice ourselves.
> Peer influences are not always negative—they can be positive too!

1 Decide if each of the situations below is an example of positive or negative peer influence. Explain why.

1 Corey's friends Matt, Ben and Aidan want him to jog around the local park every afternoon after school to practice for the interschool cross-country race.

2 Phoebe and Zoe have scratched the names of boys they like onto the bark of a tree in the forest near the school. They want Emily to do the same.

3 Connor and Liam have told Dylan he can only ride his BMX bike with them on the local bike track if he doesn't wear a helmet.

4 Shona, Mahlia and Taryn are taking tennis lessons on Wednesdays after school. They are trying to persuade Jade to join too, so they can play doubles together.

5 Mrs. Townsend's class is arranged in groups of six. One group has started throwing bits of eraser and balls of paper at other groups when she is out of the room. They want the other groups to do the same.

Scenario	Positive/Negative	Reason
1		
2		
3		
4		
5		

2 Write a positive and negative example of peer influence you have experienced.

✓	✗

3 Why do you think people give in to peer pressure?

4 How can peer influences make you feel good about yourself?

5 On the back of this sheet, add to this list of advice about resisting negative peer influences.

- *Feel good about yourself. It will help you to be strong enough to say no.*
- *Listen to yourself. It will help you to be strong enough to say no.*
- *Listen to your conscience about what is right and wrong.*

Indicator

- Considers the negative effects peer pressure has on influencing behavior and self-concept.

The Lesson

Discussion points:

- What is meant by "peer pressure" and "peer influences"?
- Can peer influences be positive and negative? How?
- List personal positive and negative peer influence experiences.
- How can you say no to a situation you know is wrong?
- How does peer influence increase self-esteem?

What to do:

- Ask for a volunteer to read the letter to the class. Students read along with the speaker.
- Students answer the comprehension questions about the letter. Some are literal and some inferential. Students may work in pairs or small groups to discuss each question before responding.
- With the class, ask students to volunteer to read out their responses to the questions. Discuss their ideas.
- In Question 7, the students respond to the letter, imagining they are Tess. Some students may need guidance with this question. These students can be read the background information on this page. Discuss with them that people with a good self-image and a strong sense of self-worth are less likely to be influenced by others. Ask them what they would tell a friend if he/she was experiencing similar things to Nicola.
- Some students may also wish to read their finished letters to the class. Discuss the similarities between the letters. What does Nicola need to help her break away from the group?

Answers:

1. Her best friend moved to a new town and so she needed new people with whom to spend her time.
2. The girls in Beccy's group don't think Computer Club is very cool.
3. Nicola is lying about where she is after school on Friday afternoons. She is also intending to lie about quitting Computer Club.
4. Possible answers: Because she doesn't have any friends after Tess moved. She wants Beccy and her group to like her. She wants to fit in.
5. Possible answers: leader, bossy, confident, dominant, reckless, bully, risk-taker, uncaring, troublesome, unafraid, etc.
6. Answers will vary   7. Teacher check

Additional Activities

- Students write about a time they experienced negative peer pressure. How did they react? Did they receive any good advice? From whom?
- Students work in small groups and make a list of positive peer influences they have experienced. They can also make a goal to help a friend or someone in their family to achieve something through their positive influences.

Display Ideas

- Enlarge Nicola's letter, mount it onto colored construction paper and display it on a large bulletin board. Students write polished versions of their reply letters (or publish them on a computer and print them out). Glue the reply letters onto colored construction paper and place them around Nicola's letter. During times when students are experiencing negative peer influences, ask them to read their and other people's letters to remind them of how to break away from negative peer influences.

Background Information

Peer pressure is allowing others to influence your thoughts and actions. People who wish to "belong" to a group are often swayed by peer pressure to follow the group's ideas and actions. Some experts believe that people who feel they belong to a group often feel more confident and their idea of self-worth increases. When in a group, people do not need to make decisions as the group tells them what to do and think.

It is important that people believe in their own self-worth and have confidence in their own thoughts, feelings and actions. People with confidence and who believe in themselves are less likely to be swayed by negative peer pressure.

Peer pressure is not always a bad thing. People can influence others to improve their behavior such as quitting a bad habit or improving their skills or a sport. Some schools have used positive peer pressure to reduce the occurrence of bullying.

Dear Tess, .

How is your new school? Have you made some new friends? Do they have Computer Club there? When is your school camp? Ours is in three weeks.

I can't believe it has been two months since you left! Things are a bit different now. I sit with Beccy's group at lunchtime. I know you are probably surprised about that, especially as we used to say that she was a bad influence on her friends, but I don't really have anyone else since you left.

At lunchtime, we generally talk about boys and our weekends. Beccy has amazing weekends! Her mom isn't home a lot so she can do whatever she likes! She wants me to go over there this weekend, but I think she will be smoking! (Don't have a heart attack just yet!)

I really want Beccy to like me, and some of the girls in her group are nice. They don't think it is very cool that I go to Computer Club, though. They keep telling me to quit. If I do, I won't be able to tell Mom and Dad. They hate it when we quit anything (and really, so do I!)

Since you left, Beccy has "gone out" with Sam, Daniel and Taj! She keeps telling me that Sam has a crush on ME now, but I don't know. After school on Fridays, we go to the park near the community center. (I tell Mom and Dad that I'm at Beccy's watching TV.) When you come for a visit at Christmas, I will tell you all about our Friday afternoons (then you CAN have a heart attack!).

Please don't show your mom this letter (or let snoopy Sasha find it!).

I hope things are going better for you. Please write to me soon. I need some advice!
Miss you,

Nicola :)
PS: Beccy is already planning a "break out" one night during camp. Aaah!

Nicola needs help. Since her best friend moved to a new town, she has lost the confidence to speak up for herself and to do what she knows is right.

Answer the questions about Nicola's letter.

1 What made Nicola join Beccy's group?

_____

_____

2 Why is Nicola considering quitting Computer Club?

_____

_____

3 Nicola is lying to her mom and dad. What is she lying about?

_____

_____

_____

4 Why do you think Nicola is giving in to peer pressure?

_____

_____

_____

5 Write five adjectives to describe Beccy.

6 How do you think Nicola is feeling about herself at the moment? How is her self-esteem?

_____

_____

7 On the back of this sheet, write Tess's reply letter to Nicola. Think about what Nicola needs to be reminded of. What advice will help her to do the right thing?

Indicator

• Identifies and categorizes scenarios into those that are bullying and those that are not.

The Lesson

Discussion points:

• Define bullying. Give examples of physical, verbal and social bullying.
• Discuss if "one-time" situations are bullying or not.
• What makes someone want to bully?
• What are the consequences of bullying—to the person bullying and the person being bullied?
• How can bullying be stopped or prevented?

What to do:

• This activity can be completed in small groups. Have students suggest examples of physical, verbal and social bullying. Stress that bullying is deliberate and repeated over time.
• Students can answer Question 1 in their groups and report back to the class to compare answers.
• Discuss Questions 2 and 3 as a class before students answer individually.

Answers:

Teacher check

Additional Activities

• Students can role-play bullying situations, then discuss what can be done to stop the situation happening again.
• Describe bullying situations seen during news bulletins, cartoons, soap operas, or drama programs on television and discuss.

Background Information

People who bully do so for many reasons. They may set out deliberately to bully and feel pleasure in bullying. It may give them a sense of power. People who bully may not necessarily lack self-esteem or be insecure. Many have average or above-average self-esteem. Their temperaments are more aggressive and they lack empathy. This can be caused by poor parenting and a lack of good role models or be a personality trait that needs fostering in a positive direction.

A summary of reasons includes:

• *They may feel upset or angry or feel they don't fit in.*
• *They want to seem tough and show off.*
• *They may get bullied themselves by family members.*
• *They're scared of getting picked on so they do it first.*
• *If they don't like themselves they may take it out on someone else.*
• *They think they will become more popular.*

Bullying can be divided into the following categories: physical, social/emotional, verbal, intimidation, written, discrimination and criminal.

Note: Criminal activity should be handled by the police or other appropriate authorities.

Bullying is deliberately hurting other people with words or actions that are repeated over a period of time. Bullying can be physical, verbal, or social. The person bullying has more power (physically or psychologically) than the person being bullied.

1 Decide if each of the situations below is a form of bullying. Explain why or why not.

1 Amber and Brittany are the only two girls in their class not invited to another's slumber party. The other girls are constantly talking about it in front of Amber and Brittany.

YES/NO

_____

_____

_____

2 Bradley is a year older than the others in his class. He finds schoolwork difficult, especially reading. Being older, he is also noticeably more physically mature than the other boys. Several students constantly tease him and call him names such as "you big idiot" and "moron."

YES/NO

_____

_____

_____

3 Dylan and his friends wait at one of the entrances to the school on most days. Some younger students leave the school by another entrance to avoid being pushed, shoved, or tripped up by the group.

YES/NO

_____

_____

_____

4 During summer vacation, Georgia had her hair cut and restyled. Her mom also bought her a new pair of the latest sneakers. Since then, some girls in her class have been whispering behind her back and laughing.

YES/NO

_____

_____

_____

5 Hannah and Kate scare younger students into giving them part of their lunch money. They threaten to pinch them and hurt them or to damage their school bags.

YES/NO

_____

_____

_____

6 Harry is nearly always the last to be chosen on a team for a gym match. Flynn told him it was because he was too fat and slow.

YES/NO

_____

_____

_____

People who bully do so for a variety of reasons. They may or may not be aware of how their bullying makes others feel.

2 Add to this list of reasons why people bully.

(a) They see it as a way of being popular.

(b) They may be jealous of the people they are bullying.

(c) It makes them feel tough or important.

(d) _____

(e) _____

(f) _____

3 How might a person feel who is being bullied? What effects could it have on him/her? Write your thoughts on the back of this sheet.

Indicators

- Understands what the term "bullying" means.
- Identifies examples of physical, verbal and social bullying.
- Considers the possible consequences of bullying.
- Uses role-play to demonstrate different strategies for dealing with bullying.

The Lesson

Discussion points:

- Is calling someone a name once bullying? Why/Why not?
- Is teasing one of your friends bullying? Explain.
- Whose responsibility is bullying in schools?
- Do you think some people are more likely to bully than others?
- Discuss where and when students feel bullying is most likely to happen at their school.
- Do you think there are any good excuses for someone to bully?
- How could you help someone who is being bullied?
- Do you think all of the strategies described on the worksheet are useful? Why/Why not? Can you suggest any more?

What to do:

- You should discuss the term "bullying" with the class before the students begin the worksheet. Also discuss the school's policy on bullying (if there is one).
- When students have answered all the questions, they should prepare their role-plays with a partner. If appropriate, these role-plays could be performed for the class and the endings discussed. Students may also like to write their own role-plays based on bullying incidents they have experienced.

Answers:

Answers will vary

Additional Activities

- Students could script their role-plays and ask another pair to perform them.
- Discuss different conflicts students have witnessed and decide as a class whether they are bullying or not.
- Brainstorm words and phrases that describe bullying. Collate the phrases to make a class definition.
- Conduct an anonymous survey among the class or younger students at the school which asks them about bullying at the school. The results could be collated and presented to the principal or other appropriate school authority.

Background Information

Bullying is very common within our schools. Students bully for many reasons: not fitting in, disliking themselves, peer pressure, wanting to show off, feeling upset or angry, or having a fear of being bullied themselves.

Bullying takes many forms, including physical abuse such as hitting, punching and tripping; verbal abuse such as name-calling, teasing and put-downs; and emotional abuse such as gossiping about someone, spreading rumors, making fun of someone, making threatening looks or gestures, and excluding or ignoring someone.

Students should be able to recognize bullying situations. They should be shown and encouraged to use strategies to cope with these situations.

Some strategies include problem-solving, role-play, tolerance, communication, conflict resolution, avoidance, learning when to ask for help and being assertive (not aggressive).

Bullying is usually deliberate, hurtful treatment that is repeated over time. Bullying can be physical (e.g., kicking someone), verbal (e.g., teasing), or social (e.g., leaving people out).

1 Write an example of each type of bullying that you have experienced or seen happening.

physical _____

_____

verbal _____

_____

social _____

_____

People who bully others need to know their bullying behavior is not allowed and it must stop. They also need to realize their actions affect people.

3 List ways that people who are bullied regularly might be affected. Consider both feelings and physical reactions.

_____

_____

_____

_____

2 What do you think the consequences should be for a person who bullies? Give your suggestions for these examples of bullying.

(a) A student who sends threatening notes to others.

_____

(b) A student who steals other students' lunch money.

_____

(c) A student who physically hurts a younger student on a regular basis.

_____

*If you are bullied, there are many different things you can do to show you will not accept the behavior of the person who is bullying you.
Some of these strategies are below.*

- Stay away from where the bullying occurs, or choose an area with lots of people.

- Boost your confidence by using positive self-talk; e.g., "I know that rumor about me isn't true."

- Ask for help (this is often appropriate after other strategies have been tried first).

- Look confident by using eye contact, good posture and clear speech.

4 Read each bullying scenario below with a partner.
Consider what you think each bullied person should do.

- *On her first day at her new school, Tamara nervously approaches a girl sitting with a group of students and asks if she can have lunch with them. The girl pretends she can't hear her. When Tamara leaves, she hears the group laughing about her.*

- *For the past two months, Liam has made Shane do his math homework for him. Liam has told Shane that if he tells anyone he will "get him" after school one day. Liam is much taller and stronger than Shane. Shane is sick of doing Liam's homework.*

- *In every physical education class, Tom manages to roughly push Amelia to the ground. His friends cheer him on. Tom always picks a time when the teacher is not looking.*

5 Prepare a role-play of each scenario with your partner, giving each a positive ending.
You can change the characters to male or female if you need to.

Indicator

- Uses conflict resolution steps to find solutions to scenarios.

The Lesson

Discussion points:

- How do you cool off when you feel angry?
- What are "I" statements? Relate some.
- What does the word "compromise" mean?
- How can a solution be acceptable to both parties?
- What do you think is meant by a "win-win" solution?
- What are some situations you have been in or seen where similar steps have been used?

What to do:

- Carefully read the steps and make sure the students understand them.
- Allow the students to read each scenario and complete their answers. Students who are encountering difficulty may wish to discuss the scenario with another student at their table. Students may discuss their answers as a group or as a whole class.
- This activity may be completed in pairs or small groups.

Answers:

Answers will vary

Additional Activities

- Students relate scenarios they have encountered to find better solutions.
- Students devise, then role-play conflict resolution scenarios.
- Have one student act as "mediator" (negotiator) to help students find appropriate solutions to their conflict situations. The mediator is NOT to provide a solution to be enforced, but to AID in finding a solution.
- Find creative and funny solutions to everyday conflict situations. Then discuss more "sensible" solutions.

Background Information

Conflict resolution is a process that directs the responsibility for solving a conflict to the people involved. Clear steps are followed to achieve a solution that suits both parties. These are:

- *defining the problem.*
- *brainstorming possible solutions.*
- *agreeing on the best solution.*
- *putting the best solution into action.*

Students should be encouraged to use conflict resolution to resolve minor conflicts such as name-calling, rumors, taking property without asking, teasing and invading personal space. The conflict resolution process teaches students that conflict need not be a negative experience, but can motivate change and provide opportunities.

Conflicts frequently occur in class, on the playground and at home. Learning to deal with conflicts calmly and sensibly, using a series of established steps, provides a fair solution for both parties.

1 Read the conflict resolution steps below.

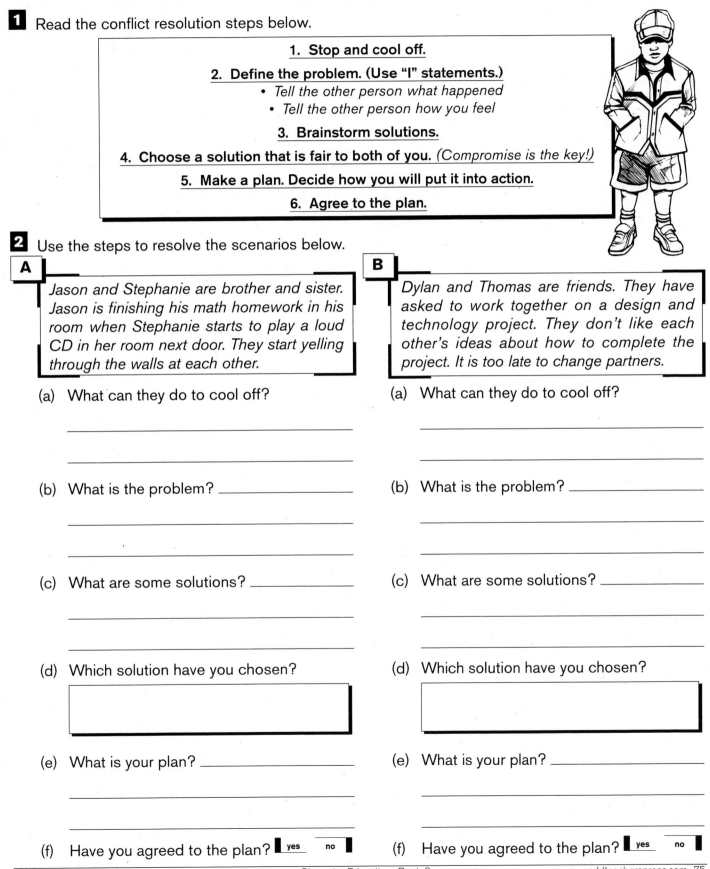

> 1. **Stop and cool off.**
>
> 2. **Define the problem. (Use "I" statements.)**
>   - *Tell the other person what happened*
>   - *Tell the other person how you feel*
>
> 3. **Brainstorm solutions.**
>
> 4. **Choose a solution that is fair to both of you.** *(Compromise is the key!)*
>
> 5. **Make a plan. Decide how you will put it into action.**
>
> 6. **Agree to the plan.**

2 Use the steps to resolve the scenarios below.

A

Jason and Stephanie are brother and sister. Jason is finishing his math homework in his room when Stephanie starts to play a loud CD in her room next door. They start yelling through the walls at each other.

(a) What can they do to cool off?

_____

_____

(b) What is the problem? _____

_____

_____

(c) What are some solutions? _____

_____

_____

(d) Which solution have you chosen?

_____

(e) What is your plan? _____

_____

_____

(f) Have you agreed to the plan? **yes** **no**

B

Dylan and Thomas are friends. They have asked to work together on a design and technology project. They don't like each other's ideas about how to complete the project. It is too late to change partners.

(a) What can they do to cool off?

_____

_____

(b) What is the problem? _____

_____

_____

(c) What are some solutions? _____

_____

_____

(d) Which solution have you chosen?

_____

(e) What is your plan? _____

_____

_____

(f) Have you agreed to the plan? **yes** **no**

Indicator

- Understands and discusses steps to resolve conflicts in a mutually acceptable way.

The Lesson

Discussion points:

- Discuss how students usually resolve minor conflicts.
- Is there more than one good way to resolve a conflict?
- Explain how each of the steps might be important in helping to solve a conflict.
- Discuss how compromise may be needed to resolve a conflict.
- Why might it be difficult to remember conflict resolution steps when you are involved in a conflict?
- Why is it important that a solution be agreed on by both parties?
- What kind of skills do you think are needed to resolve a conflict successfully?

Materials needed/Preparation:

- You will need to organize the students into groups of four or five before they begin working on the questions.

What to do:

- Read through and discuss each step as listed in the box at the top of the page. Talk about the importance of each step.
- Students move into small groups and complete Question 1. Each group will need to select a scribe and a person to report their ideas to the whole group.

Answers:

Answers will vary

Additional Activities

- Ask the students to perform role-plays of conflict resolution situations using "You" statements instead of "I" statements. What difference does this make?
- Students can write conflict scenarios based on real incidents (without using names) they have seen at the school. The scenarios could be put into a box. Pairs of students could then take a scenario and work through the conflict resolution steps to find a solution.
- Make a poster of the conflict resolution steps to display in the classroom. The students can refer to this whenever they need help to solve a conflict.

Background Information

Conflict resolution is a process that directs responsibility for solving a conflict to the people involved. Clear steps are followed to achieve a solution that suits both parties. These are:

- defining the problem.
- brainstorming possible solutions.
- agreeing on the best solution.
- putting the best solution into action.

Students should be encouraged to use conflict resolution to resolve minor conflicts, such as name-calling, spreading rumors, taking property without asking, teasing and invading personal space. The conflict resolution process teaches students that conflict need not be a negative experience, but can motivate change and provide opportunities for positive action.

Conflict resolution is a process that directs the responsibility for solving a conflict to the people involved. Finding a fair solution is the goal.

The steps used in conflict resolution are:

1. *Stop and cool off. (Count to 10, move to another part of the room, etc.)*

2. *Define the problem. (Use "I" statements or sentences beginning with "I" rather than "You.")*
   - *Tell the other person what happened (e.g., "I read your diary.").*
   - *Tell the other person how you feel (e.g., "I felt angry and disappointed when I caught you reading my diary.").*

3. *Brainstorm solutions. (Consider every idea that comes up. Keep going until you can't think of any more ideas.)*

4. *Choose a solution that is fair to both of you. (Compromise is the key!)*

5. *Make a plan. Decide how you will put it into action.*

6. *Agree to the plan. (A handshake is a good idea.)*

1 In a small group, use the conflict resolution steps to solve each of the conflicts below by considering these questions. Write notes on a separate sheet of paper.

- What could the characters do to cool off?
- What is the problem and how does each person feel? Write these as "I" statements.
- Brainstorm three possible solutions to the conflict.
- What would be a suitable plan of action for the characters to agree to?
- Which solution do you choose?

Taylor has just discovered that her friend Chelsea is responsible for telling a student in their grade some embarrassing things about her. Rumors have spread quickly and are causing Taylor to be teased. Chelsea only told the student about Taylor because she was concerned about her and wanted some advice. She is horrified that the rumors have spread. She never intended for this to happen.

Jacob's younger sister Caitlin has started following him everywhere. He can't seem to get away from her at school or at home. His parents say he should be nice to her. Jacob has tried, but Caitlin just annoys him. He has had several arguments with her about her behavior, but nothing changes. Jacob's friends have started to laugh at him. Caitlin knows she annoys Jacob, but she is lonely because her best friend has left the school. She just wants someone to talk to.

Justin has just started a new part-time job after school, stacking shelves at a supermarket. He is having problems with another boy he works with, Scott. Scott is a year older than Justin and has worked at the supermarket for six months. Justin feels that Scott bosses him around and laughs at any mistakes he makes. Scott feels he can't tell Justin anything because Justin gets angry every time he tries. Both boys want to keep their jobs.

2 Write your group's solution to each conflict.
Report your answers to the class.

Indicator

- Reads and discusses conflict resolution scenarios.

The Lesson

Discussion points:

- What is a conflict?
- Who usually resolves the conflicts at your house?
- How do you usually resolve your own conflicts?
- Is everyone happy with the solutions you have used?
- If yes–why? If not–why not?
- Are there different ways to resolve the same conflict?
- How can you make sure both parties are happy with the solution?
- Have you been in situations where you have seen someone use conflict resolution steps to solve a problem or used them yourself?
- Have you seen any situations where conflict resolution steps have not been used and the conflict has escalated to physical violence?

What to do:

- Discuss the questions above.
- Divide the class into small groups or pairs to discuss the scenarios.
- Partners or small groups may discuss one or all of the scenarios as you choose.
- Students record their solution and present it to the class in turns. A format using the conflict resolution steps may be created and used for this purpose.
- At the conclusion of each scenario, other members of the class may offer different solutions. Discuss these.

Answers:

Answers may vary as all responses are individual.

Additional Activities

- Role-play conflict situations and show how they were resolved.
- Students practice using "I" statements to express what happened and how they feel; for example, "I didn't like when you hid my bag because I was worried about my things in it, so I would prefer if you didn't touch my things without asking."
- Students practice assertive rather than passive or aggressive behavior.
- Devise a conflict resolution format for students to use when resolving conflicts.
- Students relate and discuss conflict situations from their favorite TV show and say how the characters resolved the situation. Discuss whether students agreed with the solution.

Background Information

Conflict is an occurrence in every school, workplace and home. In school, it is often the case that students faced with opposing viewpoints will go to a teacher to sort out the problem and make a final decision.

Conflict resolution is a process that directs the responsibility of solving a conflict to the students. Students learn to express their point of view, voice their ideas, and find mutually acceptable solutions.

Conflict resolution steps are to be used, if possible, before conflicts reach a physical or violent stage. Students should be encouraged to use discussion to resolve minor conflicts such as name-calling, rumors, taking property without asking, teasing and invading personal space. To resolve a conflict situation, students should feel comfortable enough to express their feelings, listen to others without feeling threatened, and negotiate a solution that suits both parties.

The conflict resolution steps are:

- Stop and cool off.
- Define the problem.
- Brainstorm solutions.
- Choose a solution that is fair to both of you.
- Make a plan.
- Agree to the plan.

Read the conflict resolution scenarios, discuss them with a partner or small group, and decide on an appropriate solution. Record your solution and present it to the class.

Jayden lets Matthew borrow his CD player for a while because his is broken. When Matthew gives it back, it does not work. Jayden is angry.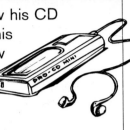

Allyssa, Breanna and Stacey are going to the school dance. Breanna wants them all to wear the same kind of clothes to the dance. However, Stacey's mom has just bought her a really cool outfit and she wants to wear that instead.

Anna and Danielle are at the shopping mall. Danielle wants Anna to hide some nail polish in her bag and leave the store without paying for it. Anna doesn't want to do it, but Danielle is her only friend.

 Sean is going into a new class at the beginning of the year. His best friend, James, will not be in the same class. He is worried and upset.

 Emily and Hayley are working on a class project together. Emily is annoyed because she seems to be doing all the work.

Jeff, Ben and Andrew are in the same group at school. Ben and Andrew often invite Jeff over to their house to play. They constantly ask Jeff if they can go to his house to play. Jeff comes from a poor family and is ashamed of his house.

Mr. Hayden is giving a math test. Stephanie and Belinda are sitting next to each other. Belinda whispers to Stephanie to ask for the answer to one of the questions.

Madeleine is having a birthday party. Her mom says that she may invite only eight children from her class. She has at least ten people that she was hoping to invite.

Jessie is always being told by her teacher how wonderful her stories are. Today the teacher told Casey that her story is really, really good.

Shane and Brad are brothers. They have decided to put their saved allowance together to buy one big thing to share. Shane wants a DVD, but Brad wants a new game.

Indicator

- Identifies and describes tolerant and intolerant behavior.

The Lesson

Discussion points:

- What does the word "tolerance" mean?
- Describe tolerant behaviors.
- Describe intolerant behaviors.
- Why do you think people show intolerant behavior towards others? (ignorance, jealousy, impatience, etc.)

What to do:

- Explain to the class that they are going to be writing a story in this lesson. The story will be about a new boy joining a class.
- Read the text at the top of the page. Discuss with the class what it might be like to join a new class. On the board, write a list of words to describe how the student might be feeling.
- Now ask the class what they think it would be like to join a new class when you are still learning the language. Add to the list on the board.
- If there are students in the class who have experienced the above, ask them if they would like to share their experiences.
- Students can work in groups to discuss the kinds of behavior the four students in the story will be exhibiting.
- Students work independently to plan and then write their stories. Some students may need guidance with their writing.
- Ask students to share their stories with the class.

Answers:

Answers will vary

Additional Activities

- Students can role-play their story with other members of the class.
- Hold a discussion on how the class reacts or would react to a new person joining. Be sensitive not to use names.
- Make a class list of tolerant behavior that can be shown toward each other, the teacher, and other staff and students in the school. Display the list in the classroom.
- When the narrative texts are at the polished stage, students could publish them on the computer and print them out. Collate the stories to make a class book that can be added to the class library and read during silent reading times.

Background Information

We live in a multicultural society. We look different. We live differently. Differences can enhance our relationships and enrich our society. Students need to be taught to recognize, appreciate and tolerate differences.

Tolerance is a skill which can reduce conflict. It is an ongoing process.

Teaching tolerance is also teaching students not to hate. Teachers can teach tolerance most effectively by modeling tolerant behavior in the classroom and on the playground. Students should be exposed to people, literature and images that are multicultural and which teach them about other faiths, ethnicities and lifestyles.

Educating students to be tolerant will:

- *promote the understanding and acceptance of people with individual differences.*
- *minimize generalizations and stereotyping.*
- *help students to understand and appreciate the differences between people.*
- *highlight the need to combat prejudice and discrimination.*

The students in class 6R have been together since First Grade. They know most things about each other and have shared lots of memories. Mrs. Riddle tells them that as of Monday a new boy will be joining the class. Antonio is from Spain, and he has only been learning English for the last few years. Mrs. Riddle tells her class that she expects them to show kindness, understanding and tolerance toward Antonio.

Write a narrative that describes how 6R reacted to Antonio on his first day. Include six main characters: Mrs. Riddle, Antonio, two students who do not show tolerance toward Antonio, and two students who are kind toward him. Resolve the situation in the last paragraph.

1 Plan your narrative text below.

Title: _____

Characters: **Mrs. Riddle and Antonio**

Student 1: _____   Character type: _____

Student 2: _____   Character type: _____

Student 3: _____   Character type: _____

Student 4: _____   Character type: _____

Setting: The classroom of 6R and _____

┌─ **Beginning:** ──────────────────────────────────────┐
│   │
│   │
│   │
│   │
└──┘

┌─ **Middle:** ───┐
│   │
│   │
│   │
│   │
└──┘

┌─ **End:** ──┐
│   │
│   │
│   │
│   │
└──┘

2 Use your plan to write the first draft of your narrative on the back of this sheet. Ask a friend to read and comment on your story before you begin the second draft.

Indicator

• Identifies and describes tolerant and intolerant behavior.

The Lesson

Discussion points:

• What does the word "tolerance" mean?

• Describe tolerant and intolerant behavior.

• Why do you think people show intolerant behavior towards others? (ignorance, jealousy, impatience)

• "Being prejudiced and discriminating against people who are different promotes hate." Discuss.

• "Tolerance is a skill which can be learned." Discuss.

• "Difference can enhance our relationships with others." Give examples.

• Where is South Africa? What do we know about it? Who is Nelson Mandela?

• What does "apartheid" mean. Does apartheid still exist in South Africa today?

What to do:

• Ask for a volunteer to read the passage at the top of the page. Enlarge the table on the worksheet onto an overhead projector transparency. Read each of the figures with the class.

• Students complete Question 1. Discuss their responses. What is shocking about the statistics in the table? How do you think the black people in South Africa lived? What was their day-to-day life like during apartheid?

• Students complete Question 2 by completing a personal response about how they feel about apartheid. Ask for volunteers to read their responses.

• Talk to the class about tolerance and peace. Explain that some people need to be educated about tolerance and need to appreciate that it is our differences that enrich our society.

• Students can work in small groups or pairs to complete Question 3. They will need to consider ways they can promote tolerance at school. Once completed, ask for ideas from the class. Make a list somewhere permanent in the classroom. Students can be reminded of this list when the class or members of the school are experiencing conflict.

Answers:

1. (a) 14.5 million
   (b) white (74% more land than the blacks)
   (c) very small chance considering there was one doctor for every 44,000 black people
2. Answers will vary as responses are personal
3. Teacher check

Additional Activities

• Students create posters to promote tolerance in the school. Each group can create one which can be displayed in a public area such as in the hall, library, office, or outside (if laminated).

• Some students may be interested to know about the state of South Africa today. Find a web site that is suitable for students and bookmark it. Allow interested students to view the web site and compile a report on how things have changed in South Africa since apartheid was abolished. Students can write a short oral report to present to the class about South Africa.

Background Information

We live in a multicultural society. We look different. We live differently. Differences can enhance our relationships and enrich our society. Students need to be taught to recognize, appreciate and tolerate differences.

Tolerance is a skill which can reduce conflict. It is an ongoing process.

Teaching tolerance is also teaching students not to hate. Teachers can teach tolerance most effectively by modeling tolerant behavior in the classroom and on the playground. Students should be exposed to people, literature and images that are multicultural and which teach them about other faiths, ethnicities and lifestyles.

Educating students to be tolerant will:

• *promote the understanding and acceptance of people with individual differences.*

• *minimize generalizations and stereotyping.*

• *help students to understand and appreciate the differences between people.*

• *highlight the need to combat prejudice and discrimination.*

Apartheid *n. racial segregation*

In 1948, apartheid laws were enacted in South Africa and discrimination against a person because of his/her skin color became legal.

Laws were created and enforced to stop marriage between "whites" and "non-whites" and many jobs were advertised as "white-only."

One of the main aims of apartheid was to give preferential treatment to whites. Did it succeed?

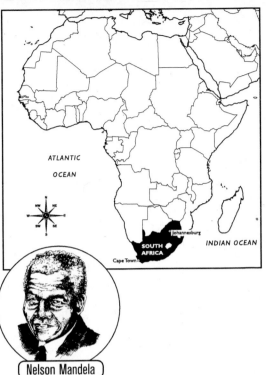

Apartheid and the People of South Africa – 1978	Blacks	Whites
Population	19 million	4.5 million
Land allocation	13 percent	87 percent
Maximum income	360 rand	750 rand
Doctors per head of population	1 per 44,000	1 per 400
Infant mortality rate	40%	2.7%
Yearly expenditure on education per student	$45	$696
Teacher–student ratio	1 per 60	1 per 22

Nelson Mandela

1 Study the table above and answer these questions.

(a) How many more black people than white people were there in South Africa in 1978?

_____

(b) Who had more land? _____

(c) If you were a black person in South Africa and became sick, how likely was it that you would see a doctor? Why?

_____

_____

2 Discrimination against people because of their skin color was legal and acceptable during apartheid. How does that make you feel?

_____

_____

3 Tolerance is being taught today in schools and workplaces in many countries. People need to understand and appreciate that it is our differences that make us special and enrich our society. Tolerance is a skill which can reduce conflict and promote peace.

Think of ways you can help to promote tolerance and peace in your school.

Indicators

- Recognizes actions that are disrespectful.
- Considers ways to act respectfully toward others.
- Identifies ways of showing respect to other people.

The Lesson

Discussion points:

- What does "respect" mean?
- Whom do you respect the most? Why?
- Who shows you respect?
- "It is important that we respect ourselves." Discuss.

What to do:

- Divide the class into small groups. The groups discuss each scenario.

  They can discuss: Who is being disrespectful?
  Who is not being respected?
  How are they not being respected?

- In groups or independently, the students write ways they can show respect to the people in their lives.
- Discuss with the class why it is important to have self-respect. Explain that we should all treat others the way we expect to be treated ourselves.
- Independently, the students complete Question 2. Ask the students who need guidance to think about the following:
  – How do you like to be spoken to?
  – Do you expect people to act fairly towards you?
  – Do you expect people to tell you the truth?

Answers:

Answers will vary

Additional Activities

- Students discuss each scenario and decide what they think the consequence for each behavior should be. Ask the groups to share their responses with the class. Are there discrepancies between the level of punishment? Why? Discuss.
- Students can role-play some of the scenarios on the worksheet. They can then perform role-plays where the person not being respectfully treated confronts the other person and asks why they are acting the way they are.
- In groups, students create posters with the heading RESPECT! They can use text, pictures, art materials, etc., to present their own visions of what respect means to them.

Background Information

Treating others with respect makes the world a nicer place. We show respect to others when we treat them the way we would like to be treated.

A respectful person:

- *is courteous and polite.*
- *listens to what others have to say.*
- *doesn't insult, judge, or make fun of people, call them names, or bully them.*
- *doesn't judge people before he/she gets to know them.*
- *is sensitive to the feelings of others.*
- *doesn't put pressure on someone to do something he/she doesn't want to do.*

1 Read each scenario. Discuss it with your group. Consider how you can act respectfully toward the people in your life. Write your ideas in each box.

Jason comes home from school in a bad mood. He walks into the house, drops his bag in the middle of the hall and walks to the fridge. He ignores his mom, who asks him how his day was. He takes a snack from the fridge, walks to his room and shuts the door.	**I can respect my family by ....**
Three Grade 6 boys are sitting at the back of the bus. They use markers to draw on the back of the seats and on the wall. The bus driver cannot see what they are doing.	**I can respect my community by ...**
Lizzy is at her grandma's 70th birthday party. She has her CD Walkman® with her and listens to her music for most of the day. Some of her grandma's friends try to speak to her, but Lizzy just shouts "What?" at them.	**I can respect the elderly by ...**
Nanthini tells her friend, Sophie, something in confidence. A few days later, Nanthini hears a few other girls from her class whispering about her and laughing.	**I can respect my friends by ...**
Philip thought he was playing an amazing game of soccer until the coach asked him to come off the field. Philip was furious as he walked towards the bench and yelled at his coach that he needed glasses.	**I can respect my coach/teacher by ...**

Showing respect for yourself and others is an important quality to develop.
We show respect for others when we treat them the way we like to be treated ourselves.

2 Describe how you expect to be treated by others. _____

_____

_____

Indicators

- Recognizes actions that are disrespectful.
- Considers ways to act respectfully towards others.
- Identifies ways of showing respect to other people.

The Lesson

Discussion points:

- What does "respect" mean?
- Whom do you respect the most? Why?
- Who shows you respect?
- "It is important that we respect ourselves." Discuss.

What to do:

- Divide the class into small groups. Each group reads the poem together.
- Students discuss Questions 1 to 3, then write responses independently.
- Students can work in pairs or small groups to create their piece for Question 4. Discuss each option with the class. Explain that their responses will be displayed around the school (or if a role-play or debate, presented in front of the class).
- Students will need time to work on their piece, and to polish and perform it.
- After each piece has been displayed or performed, discuss it with the class. Ask the students what they have learned from each piece of work.

Answers:

Answers will vary

Additional Activities

- Students write a poem about respect. They can focus on respecting others or respecting themselves.
  Poems can be acrostic, rhyming, narrative, haiku, etc.
- Discuss with the class what can be done if you feel you are not being respected. How can a person change to receive more respect from others?
  - Show respect to others (being considerate, caring, tolerant, etc.).
  - Try being more assertive (use "I" statements, etc.)

Display Ideas

- Groups who have completed work for Question 4 that can be displayed should ask if their work can be put on show in a public area, such as the library or office entrance.
- Groups who have performance pieces could repeat their performance to a wider audience, such as a class in the upper levels or, if appropriate, the whole school.

Background Information

Treating others with respect makes the world a nicer place. We show respect to others when we treat them the way we would like to be treated.

A respectful person:

- *is courteous and polite.*
- *listens to what others have to say.*
- *doesn't insult, judge, make fun of people, call them names, or bully them.*
- *doesn't judge people before getting to know them.*
- *is sensitive to the feelings of others.*
- *doesn't put pressure on people to do something they don't want to do.*

RESPECT

When you ignore me,
When you call me names,
When you judge me because of the
clothes I wear
or the way I wear my hair,
When you don't care when I'm hurt
... on the inside,
When you make me do things
I don't want to do, then laugh about it
... you make me feel small.
I deserve to be treated better than this.
I speak to you politely and
listen when you talk.
I never judge or bully you.
I care when you are sad.
Treat me the way I treat you!
Give me the respect I deserve.

1 Read the poem.
Who do you think the writer is speaking about?
What makes you think that?

_____

_____

_____

_____

_____

_____

_____

_____

_____

_____

2 What type of person do you think the writer is? Write adjectives to describe him/her.

_____

3 In the poem, the writer says that he/she feels "small." Have you ever felt like this?
Describe your experience.

_____

_____

_____

4 We show respect to others when we treat them the way we would like to be treated.

Treating others with respect makes the world a nicer place.

(a) Read the phrase above. In your groups, choose a way to present this message to an audience.
There are some ideas on the right.

(b) Plan your piece. Speak to your teacher about the resources you might
need (such as the Internet, craft materials, video camera, or costumes).

(c) Prepare your piece.

(d) Polish your piece until it is ready for display or performance.

(e) Evaluate your work. How happy are you with the finished product?

• *poem*
• *short play*
• *poster*
• *news report/article*
• *creative story*
• *children's book*
• *web page*
• *debate*
• *historical piece*
• *documentary*

○————————————○————————————○
unsatisfactory   needs improving   perfection

Indicator

- Considers possible consequences in taking risks.

The Lesson

Discussion points:

- What is a risk? How can you decide whether to take a risk or not?
- Name some of the everyday risks you take at school.
- What is the biggest risk you have taken? Was it worth it?
- Discuss different kinds of risks; e.g., physical, emotional, financial.
- Have you ever been talked into taking a risk you would have rather not taken? Explain.

What to do:

- Discuss the term "risk" and what it means. Talk to the students about how people are often afraid to take risks because they are frightened of failing or embarrassing themselves. Emphasize that there are many different types of risks.
- Read the text at the top of the page. Make sure students understand what is meant by a positive and a negative outcome.
- Ask students to complete Question 1. They could then compare their answers to a partner's. A tally of how many students answered "yes" or "no" to each scenario could be taken.
- Ask students to complete Questions 2 and 3. Afterwards, students could role-play their answers to Question 2 with a partner, making sure they clearly act the feelings given. Answers to Question 3 could also be discussed and shared to see how many students wrote similar answers.

Answers:

Answers will vary

Additional Activities

- Play drama games that involve an element of risk; e.g., blindfold games. Discuss how they made students feel.
- Ask students to create a flow chart of the thought process they can follow when they are considering taking a risk.

Background Information

People who take few calculated risks often find failure more difficult to deal with than do people who take risks. Students should therefore be encouraged to take calculated risks. Establishing a caring classroom environment will help them to feel more confident about doing this.

> Taking a risk means to do something that may or may not have a positive outcome. People take risks every day. Most of these are small risks that neither cause us harm nor put us in a difficult situation. However, some risks can have a major influence on our lives.
>
> *Before taking any risk, it is important to consider the likely outcomes.*

1 Consider a likely positive and a likely negative outcome for each of these risks.

Risk	Positive outcome	Negative outcome	Would I take the risk?
You consider answering a question in class. You are almost sure you know the correct answer.			
You are new to a school. You consider walking up to a group of students to introduce yourself.			
Your drama teacher asks you to take the main part in a play. You feel nervous, but you love drama and want to be an actor.			

2 Describe a time when you took a risk that had a positive outcome.
List your feelings before and after you took the risk.

Feelings before	Risk and outcome	Feelings after

3 Sometimes it is unwise to take a risk because it is almost certain it will have negative consequences for you or someone else. Give an example of a risk you wouldn't consider taking for this reason.

Indicator

- Follows decision-making steps to make a decision.

The Lesson

Discussion points:

- Do you worry about what your friends will think if your decision is different from theirs?
- Do you sometimes disagree with the decisions of your friends?
- Have you ever made a decision and regretted it later? Relate some of these. (optional)
- Have you ever hurt someone by making the wrong decision?
- Have you ever made a difficult decision and been very pleased with your choice later?
- What are some things you could never do? Why would you never do them? (optional)

What to do:

- Read the opening paragraph and Question 1 with the students. Discuss the steps.
- Discuss the points above with the students before asking them to read the scenario and to answer Question 2 independently. Students may discuss their answers with the remainder of the class upon completion. You may collect the students' work and read it for their own information.

Answers:

Answers will vary

Additional Activities

- Read other scenarios and discuss possible decisions.
- Decide who are the major decision makers at home, among your friends, at school, and at your leisure groups (soccer team, scouts, karate class, music class, etc.).
- Brainstorm a list of things or people who influence your opinions or decisions.
- Brainstorm a list of positive aspects of making a wrong decision, such as learning from experiences and hoping to not repeat the same mistakes again.

Background Information

It is important that students learn to stop and think about whether something is right or wrong before making a choice. The steps for decision making are:

- *define the problem.*
- *brainstorm possible solutions.*
- *evaluate the ideas (consider all consequences).*
- *decide on a solution and carry it out.*

Some decisions are easy to make, such as choosing between two types of takeout foods, while others are more difficult. Decisions which involve a choice between right and wrong or which could have bad consequences are not easy to make.

1 Before making a difficult decision, it is important to stop and think about the results of making a particular choice. Ask yourself these questions before deciding.

- Do I feel good about this decision?

- Will I hurt someone by doing this?

- Will it be fair?

- How would I feel if someone did this to me?

- Have I been told before not to do this?

- How do I really feel about doing this, deep down?

- Will I still feel good about my decision later?

- Would the adults I respect agree with my choice?

IF YOU ARE STILL UNSURE, TALK TO SOMEONE YOU TRUST!

2 Read the scenario below and complete the decision-making questions.

Sasha and Chloe are in the "cool" group at school. They wear the most fashionable clothes to the dance and the shopping mall. They have the latest CDs and DVDs. Their hair always looks great. They are both really good at English and math and are very popular with the teachers and the other students in the class. The elections for class monitors are announced and Aimee, who is very shy, would really like to be nominated. She doesn't know whether to put her hand up to be considered, because she thinks that everyone will vote for Sasha and Chloe.

What should Aimee do?

(a) What is Aimee's problem? _____

_____

_____

(b) What are her choices? _____

_____

_____

_____

(c) Look at the possible choices. Write one consequence for each of the decisions she has to make.

_____

_____

_____

_____

_____

(d) What do you think her decision should be?

Why? _____

_____

_____

Indicators

- Understands and uses a plan to make decisions.
- Considers some important decisions he/she has made.

The Lesson

Discussion points:

- What are some of the most important decisions you have had to make?
- What do you think will be the most important decisions you will have to make in the future?
- What does it mean to be "indecisive"? Is it a problem?
- What kinds of jobs require positive decision-making on a regular basis?
- How do you feel when you make a decision that turns out to be the "right" one?
- How do you feel when you make a decision that turns out to be the "wrong" one?

What to do:

- Before the students begin the worksheet, discuss some examples of difficult decisions students in the class have had to make and how they felt about them.
- Students can compare their answers to Question 2 with a partner.
- After students have completed Question 4, make a tally of the most common decisions described. These could be used as topics of discussion with the class.

Answers:

Answers will vary

Additional Activities

- Students can invent their own "problem page" letters asking for advice on decisions that have to be made. They can write replies to their own letters or ask a partner to reply.
- The students can write an explanation or a procedure of the decision-making plan suitable for a younger student to understand. The piece of writing should include appropriate examples.

Background Information

It is important that students learn to stop and think about whether something is right or wrong before making a choice. The steps for decision-making are:

- *define the problem.*
- *brainstorm possible solutions.*
- *evaluate the ideas (consider all consequences).*
- *decide on a solution and carry it out.*

Making decisions is not always easy. There are usually consequences that can affect not only your own life, but the lives of others as well. These can be positive or negative. Using a plan when you are faced with an important decision can be helpful.

A useful plan to follow is:

define the problem → explore the options → consider the consequences → make a decision

1 What is a "consequence"?
Give an example of a positive consequence and a negative consequence.

_____

_____

2 Imagine you see this page in a magazine. If you were each of these people, what decision would you make? Use the plan to help you make a final decision. Write notes to show your thoughts.

Dear Problem Solver,

I have been playing hockey for six years and I want to be an Olympic athlete one day. There is an important match coming up that my team is going to play in, but I have a decision to make. My best friend has asked me to travel to Europe with her family for three weeks and my parents have said I can go! And you guessed it–the match is right in the middle of the trip. What do you think I should do? I don't want to let the team down, but my parents couldn't afford to take our whole family to Europe. I love traveling and am excited at the thought of the trip.

Dear Problem Solver,

A few days ago, one of my friends told me he had a secret that I had to promise not to tell anyone. After I promised, he told me he had started shoplifting because the group he is now hanging around with forced him to. He is terrified of being caught by the police. I want to help him, but I don't want to break my promise by telling anyone. He is a good friend and I don't want to lose him. Besides, the group might start bullying me if they found out I said something. What should I do?

Options and consequences

Final decision

Options and consequences

Final decision

3 Describe a difficult decision you wished you had made differently and explain why.

_____

_____

4 Describe a difficult decision you are pleased you made and explain why.

_____

_____

5 On a separate sheet of paper, use the plan to make a decision on an issue that may affect you in the next few years; e.g., what subjects you will take next year.

Indicators

- Understands the meaning of values.
- Identifies some of his/her own values.

The Lesson

Discussion points:

- What do you think a value is?
- What kinds of things do you value?
- "Sometimes not knowing what our values are can lead us to do things we don't really want to do." Discuss.

Materials Needed/Preparation:

- The day before the lesson, ask students to think about who their heroes are and whom they admire. Ask the class to bring in some information and (if possible) pictures of that person for the following lesson. This may require students to have access to the school's computers to download information from the Internet. (Be aware of which personalities they have chosen before giving them access to the Internet.)

What to do:

- Students complete Questions 1 and 2 independently. Ask students to volunteer to read their responses to the class.
- Discuss with the students that it is important to think about what we value. We can often have our values challenged by our peers, and so we need to feel confident about our values.
- Students complete an email to a penpal describing themselves, their interests and their values. Explain that this piece of writing is personal and does not have to be shared with the class. Some students may wish to volunteer to read their emails to the class. Discuss what values the email is expressing.

Answers:

Answers will vary

Additional Activities

- Students choose a style of poetry and write a poem to express what they value. Options could include an acrostic, a shape, or rhyming poem.
- Write a narrative involving a group of four students. One of the students has his/her values challenged by the other group members. Does he/she give in and follow the group, or does he/she stand up for his/her values and ignore the group?

  The story must have a beginning, middle and end, and have a well-defined central character.
- Students present a polished piece of poetry or narrative text on colored construction paper for display.

Background Information

Our values create the basis for how we lead our lives. When we have confidence in ourselves and strong values, it is easier to do things that are right for us. Those who have weaker values can be easily led and may end up doing things they don't really want to do.

You can discuss some values with students, such as honesty, generosity, tolerance and kindness. They may also like to discuss other things people value, like pets, music and the environment.

©World Teachers Press®

1 Do you have a hero or someone whom you admire and would like to be like? Who is it, and what is it about that person that you admire? Write about your hero below, and either find and glue or sketch a picture of him/her in the box.

_____

_____

_____

_____

_____

_____

_____

2 Think about your friends. What is it about them that you like and admire? Do they have any similar qualities? Complete the sentence.

The qualities my friends have include: _____

_____

_____

Remember that your values are what you consider to be important in life. Sometimes it can be hard to know what we value. By completing these activities, you are helping to identify your values.

3 Your teacher has just returned from a vacation to another country where she visited a local school and swapped email addresses with the sixth grade teacher there. You have been assigned a student from the class to correspond with and must now create an email telling him/her about yourself. Include in your email:

your interests   _your goals (career and others)_   _what is important to you_

To:

From:

Subject:

(**Send**)

Indicators

- Understands the meaning of values.
- Identifies some of his/her own values.

The Lesson

Discussion points:

- What do you think a value is?
- What kinds of things do you value?
- "Sometimes not knowing what our values are can lead us to do things we don't really want to do." Discuss.
- "Just be yourself!" Discuss.
- What do you think your parents value? What do your friends value?

Materials needed/Preparation:

- Prior to this lesson, look at web sites of famous people. Print or bookmark these to show the class before they begin Question 2. If possible, find a web site about someone who has died to show the students how the text is written in the past tense and in the third person; for example, "He was an adventurer who loved…", etc.
- Site search: Charles M. Schulz, Walt Disney, Jim Henson, etc.

What to do:

- Discuss with the class that our values are what we think is important and this can be shown by our behavior. Students will write a web page about themselves, commenting on their lives and what they have achieved. A student may write that he/she became a famous soccer star, showing that he/she values hard work, practice, perseverance and achieving success. Another student may write that he wrote a bestselling book, showing that he values knowledge, hard work, etc.
- Show the students examples of other web pages, either on the computer or with printouts. Explain that the text should sound as if it is written by someone else. The students will write in the third person ("He/She," not "I"). The web text should also be written in the past tense.
- Students can share their work with the class. With each one, try to bring out what the achievements show. What does each student value?

Answers:

Teacher check

Additional Activities

- Students choose a "hero" of theirs and search the Internet to see if he/she has a web site. They review the web site and make comments on what they believe the person values. Are the values expressed similar to their own?
- Students write a role-play between two people who have very different values. The people are in conflict but resolve the situation in the end through compromise and negotiation.

Display Ideas

- Students create final copies of their web sites and display them on colored construction paper.

Background Information

Our values create the basis for how we lead our lives. When we have confidence in ourselves and strong values, it is easier to do things that are right for us. Those who have weaker values can be led easily and may end up doing things they don't really want to do.

You can discuss some values with students, such as honesty, generosity, tolerance and kindness. They may also like to discuss other things people value, like pets, music, the environment, etc.

Your great-granddaughter is surfing the Net and finds a web site all about you!

Create your web site below. Think about:

- How you are described.
- What you looked like as an adult.

- Your teenage years.
- What you achieved in your life.

Remember to write in the third person (he/she) and in the past tense (lived, achieved, etc.)

| File | Edit | View | Go | Favorites | Tools | Window | Help | ☉Super Searcher |

═ @ the life of ... ═

| ◀ Back | ▶ Forward | ✖ Stop | ↻ Refresh | 🏠 Home | ✉ Mail | 🖨 Print |

Address: @http://www. ▶ **go**

The life of

Click here

- The early years
- Teens
- Family life
- Achievements
- The final years
- Epitaph

ORDER NOW

- Biography (10% discount)
- Autobiography
- CD-Rom of autobiography with personal photographs

Search
Advanced search
Search year
Image database
Send Email

⊕⊖○   Teens

⊕⊖○   Achievements

Indicators

- Reads a poem about keeping the environment healthy.
- Offers suggestions about how to keep the environment healthy.

The Lesson

Discussion points:

- What is meant by "our environment"?
- How does the environment become unhealthy?
- How can we keep it healthy or make it better?
- What does "recycle" mean?
- How can we reuse our resources?
- How does it help our environment to plant trees?
- What are some ways to conserve water?
- What does it mean to "replenish the land"? How can we do this?

What to do:

- Discuss the points above.
- Read the poem with the students and discuss any unknown words.
- Students may discuss answers for Question 1 with a friend and complete the boxes, or work independently.
- Students answer Question 2 independently and may share their answers with the class. You may list answers to Question 2 on the board or on a sheet of poster board for display.
- Question 3 may be given as a homework project or completed in class. Completed posters may be displayed in the room or on the windows to encourage others to look after their environment.

Answers:

Answers will vary since responses are individual.

Additional Activities

- Investigate local conservation areas where students can be involved.
- Make a world shape during art and craft activities; add arms and legs to make it look "human" and write a slogan promoting a healthy environment on it.
- Begin a worm farm at the school to encourage the reuse of school lunch scraps.
- Start a compost heap at your house.
- Decorate the school trash cans; make them very visible, so students always remember to put their garbage in them.
- Hold a "package-free" day and ask students to bring their snacks and lunches without wrapping. Count and record the amounts and types of garbage left; compare to the following day, when packaging will be back to normal.
- Reward students who clean up without asking.
- Hold a "Cleanest Classroom" competition and reward the class which keeps the area outside their classroom the tidiest.
- Adopt a school garden to weed, water and keep tidy.

Background Information

Our earth and its resources are finite. We need to encourage students from an early age to look after the environment and keep it healthy. Strategies need to be taught and reinforced to allow students to do their part to help the environment. Students shouldn't be discouraged and think that the task is too difficult for their efforts to have any impact. Every person can make a difference. Students can take responsibility for their own yard, classroom, school playground and local environment. Students can be involved in tree-planting days and forest-care days.

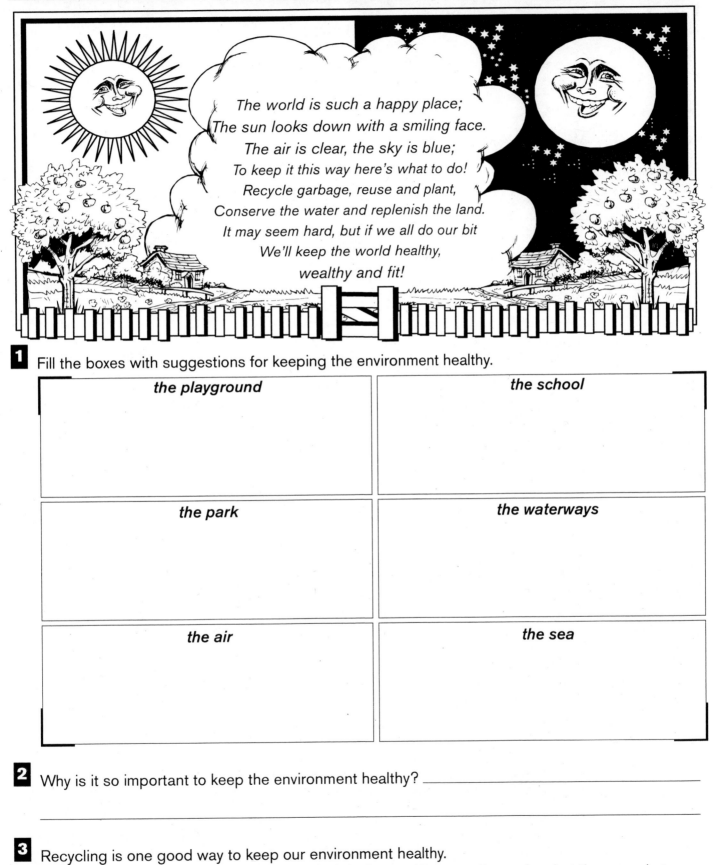

The world is such a happy place;
The sun looks down with a smiling face.
The air is clear, the sky is blue;
To keep it this way here's what to do!
Recycle garbage, reuse and plant,
Conserve the water and replenish the land.
It may seem hard, but if we all do our bit
We'll keep the world healthy,
wealthy and fit!

1 Fill the boxes with suggestions for keeping the environment healthy.

the playground	the school

the park	the waterways

the air	the sea

2 Why is it so important to keep the environment healthy? _____

_____

3 Recycling is one good way to keep our environment healthy.
On a separate sheet of paper, research and design a poster to tell people what they can do to help.

Indicators

- Demonstrates an understanding that commitment to a project is part of being responsible.
- Considers carefully a project he/she would like to participate in and plans his/her involvement in detail.

The Lesson

Discussion points:

- What does it mean to be "responsible"?
- What are the benefits of being responsible?
- Do you think people are responsible when it comes to the environment? Explain.
- Why does commitment play such a big part in being responsible?
- Do you think the level of importance of something plays a part in how much energy you put into a project? Explain.

Materials needed/Preparation:

- Organize students into groups of five or six
- Butcher paper for each group
- Internet, telephone directories, telephone, local maps

What to do:

- Begin by developing an understanding about what it is to be responsible. Organize the class into small groups; give each group a piece of butcher paper for recording the group's responses to the first discussion question.
- Ask students to consider the benefits of being responsible, such as freedom, self-respect, decision making, increases self-esteem, etc. Share these ideas with the whole class.
- Read the Background Information to the students and discuss the third Discussion point. Students will have varying ideas on this topic, depending on whether or not they are involved in groups which are environmentally aware or whether or not they are environmentally aware themselves.
- Direct students to the worksheet. Explain to the students that this activity requires them to carefully consider an environmental project in their local area pertaining to the care and recovery of local waterways. If your local environment does not lend itself to this topic, a study of water use in the home and school could be undertaken.
- Students complete Questions 1 to 5 on the worksheet. Students can access the Internet or telephone services to make contact with organizations in order to fully research the project he/she might like to participate in. Ensure students have adequate practice at gathering information over the telephone (polite introduction, explanation of the project and appropriate questions to ask, polite salutation).
- Discuss, as a whole class, the final two Discussion points. Ensure students have an understanding of the importance of being committed to a project (turning up on time, maintaining enthusiasm, etc.) as a group comes to depend and rely on you.
- Students can then complete the remainder of the worksheet.

Answers:

Answers will vary

Additional Activities

- Follow through with the project and encourage students to report their experiences to the class via photographs, talks, posters, charts, guest speakers and so on.
- Students can keep a diary of their thoughts and feelings and how they feel the experience has helped them as a person.
- Students can collaborate on an environmental project within the school. They need to write a directive, including what they intend to do, the time they will be able to dedicate to the project, who will help them with the project, the outcome they wish to achieve and by when it is to be achieved.

Background Information

In recent years, concern regarding our waterways has increased, and people are becoming more aware of the problems facing our waterways. The media is presenting the public with new information on a daily basis about how they can help to protect the quality of water in our rivers, streams, lakes and ponds. There are many opportunities for the general public, school students and organizations to become involved in programs to improve our waterways; for example, testing water quality, recording wildlife found in particular locations, or clearing garbage out of rivers and lakes. The groups involved in these programs monitor their waterways, and over time can determine whether the environmental quality of the waterway is improving, declining, or being maintained. Many groups have successfully implemented new projects such as fencing areas of riverbanks, eradicating weeds and reducing the use of pesticides and other pollutants to improve the quality of their local waterways.

Looking after your environment means being responsible.

1 Think about and decide what you would like to do to improve your local waterways.

2 How can you find out more information about what you would like to do? (Use resources.)

3 Is there a suitable project already running? ▋ yes ▋ no ▋

4
Name of project: _____   Who runs it: _____

Telephone: _____   Email: _____

Where: _____   When: _____

What: _____

_____

_____

5 What will be your role in the project?

6 How much time will you dedicate to the project? (Be specific about hours and days each week or month. Also consider other commitments you already have.)

My time:

School time:

7 How do you plan to follow through with your commitment?

8 How long do you plan to work on this project?

9 Are you going to do this project …

▋ independently?   ▋ with friends? ▋

▋ with family?   as a class? ▋

10 Explain why this project is important to you and how you will feel by participating.

_____

Indicator

• Describes actions to address an issue affecting the environment.

The Lesson

Discussion points:

• What local environmental issues affect our health?
• What global environmental issues affect us?
• What strategies have already been used?
• How can you make a difference?

What to do:

• Have students work in small groups to discuss environmental issues that affect our health in some way. Issues may include: pollution, community drug problems (including alcohol and illegal drugs), unsafe areas, traffic, lack of recreational facilities. Ask students to devise strategies to solve a specific issue. Reports can be presented to the class or displayed.

• With students working in pairs or small groups, ask them to discuss global environmental issues. These could include hunger, poverty, destruction of the rainforests, global warming, AIDS, or pollution. Provide opportunities for students to use the Internet and library facilities to research the specific issue. Findings could be presented in a report to the class.

Answers:

Teacher check

Additional Activities

• Using the issues raised, create a debating situation where groups are involved in presenting for and against arguments.

• Students can write letters to the editor of a newspaper, outlining the issue they are researching and suggest strategies.

Background Information

Many people have come to realize that one of our basic needs in life is to have a healthy environment. We can choose to become involved in making changes to our lifestyle so the things we do decrease the detrimental impact on the environment. We can also undertake activities to improve the environment.

For young people, getting involved with tree planting, cleaning up garbage and fund-raising for threatened species are just a few easy ways to learn how to care responsibly for the natural world.

1 In your group discuss environmental issues that may have an effect on health.
Choose one issue and describe how it could be resolved.

Describe the issue	
What goal do you want to achieve?	
Who is affected?	
Where is the problem area located?	
What strategies will you use to help solve the problem?	
What resources will you need?	
What will the final result be?	
Illustrate before and after	

2 Use the Internet to research a current global issue that affects the environment.
Use the same headings as above to record your findings.

Sample Page from World Teachers Press' *Healthy Choices, Gr. 6-8* (www.didax.com/2-5255)

A HEALTHY DIET

What Is a Healthy Diet?

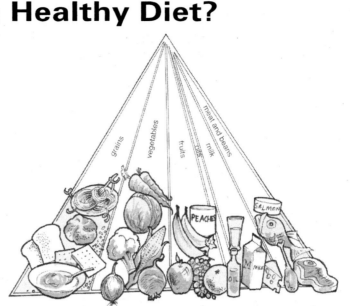

Have you ever heard the saying "You are what you eat"? It's true! Sticking to a healthy diet means you will look and feel your best. But how do we know exactly what a healthy diet is? Using the Healthy Eating Guide *is a good way to help us understand this. It shows the proportion of different types of foods we should eat each day.*

- *The types of foods you should eat the most are bread, cereal, rice, pasta and noodles. These foods are excellent sources of carbohydrates.*

- *Vegetables, legumes and fruit are given an important emphasis on the diagram because they are loaded with vitamins, minerals, carbohydrates and fiber.*

- *Milk, yogurt and cheese are important because they are an excellent source of calcium and protein.*

- *Lean meat, fish, poultry, eggs, nuts and legumes provide us with protein, iron and zinc.*

- *Fats, oils and sugars are not listed in the diagram as, separately, they are not essential to our diet and should only be eaten in small amounts.*

Answer these questions.

1. Use an encyclopedia to write one way each of these assists our bodies.

    (a) carbohydrates _____

    (b) fiber _____

    (c) calcium _____

    (d) protein _____

    (e) iron _____

    (f) zinc _____

2. Using the *Healthy Eating Guide*, plan a day's meals and snacks that you would enjoy.

Breakfast	Snack	Lunch	Snack	Dinner

HEALTH CHALLENGE

Each day for one week, try eating a healthy food you have never tried.